D1092848

WITHDRAWN

THE
PAUL HAMLYN
LIBRARY

DONATED BY
THE PAUL HAMLYN
FOUNDATION
TO THE
BRITISH MUSEUM

opened December 2000

A GOD AND HIS GIFTS

BY THE SAME AUTHOR:

PASTORS AND MASTERS

BROTHERS AND SISTERS

MEN AND WIVES

MORE WOMEN THAN MEN

A HOUSE AND ITS HEAD

DAUGHTERS AND SONS

A FAMILY AND A FORTUNE

PARENTS AND CHILDREN

ELDERS AND BETTERS

MANSERVANT AND MAIDSERVANT

TWO WORLDS AND THEIR WAYS

DARKNESS AND DAY

THE PRESENT AND THE PAST

MOTHER AND SON

A FATHER AND HIS FATE

A HERITAGE AND ITS HISTORY

THE MIGHTY AND THEIR FALL

THE LAST AND THE FIRST

A GOD AND HIS GIFTS

by

I. COMPTON-BURNETT

LONDON
VICTOR GOLLANCZ LIMITED
1979

© I. Compton-Burnett 1963

ISBN 0 575 02578 6

First published 1963
Reissued 1979

Printed in Great Britain at
The Camelot Press Ltd, Southampton

CHAPTER I

"I will ask you once more. It is the last time. Will you or will you not?"

"I will not. It is also the last time. It must be the last."

"You will not give me your reasons?"

"I will give you one. You have too much. Your house and your land. Your parents and your sister. Your sister who is also your friend. Your work and your growing name. I like things to be on a moderate scale. To have them in my hands and not be held by them."

"That is not the only reason. There must be a deeper one."

"There is. And it may be deep. I do not want to marry. I seldom say so, to be disbelieved."

"You don't feel that marriage would mean a fuller life?"

"I don't want the things it would be full of. Light words are sometimes true."

"Then there must be a change. I do want to marry. I want to have descendants. I want to hand down my name. I could not keep up our relation under a wife's eyes. It has escaped my parents."

"Your father I daresay. What about your mother?"

"I am not sure. It is hard to know."

"It has not escaped her, or you would know. Silence has its use."

The speaker's indifference to convention appeared in her clothes, her cottage, and her habit of looking full at her companion and voicing her thought. She was a short, fair woman of about thirty, with a deep voice, a strongly cut face, and calm eyes that were said to see more than other people's, and sometimes did. Her companion was a large, dark man, with solid, shapely features, heavy, gentle, nervous hands, strong, sudden movements and a look of smouldering force. He ignored convention in another way, and in one that was his own. A consciousness of being a known and regarded figure showed in his dress and his bearing, and was almost undisguised. The breach of family tradition involved in his leading a writer's life in addition to a landowner's, enhanced him in his own eyes and supported his conception of himself.

"Well, this is a last occasion. It becomes one. It is what you choose."

"And what you do. I think you will be happy. And I hope she will. That is where the question lies."

"If I marry her, she should be. I will do my part."

"It will be easier than hers. I wonder if you know it."

"Hers cannot be what yours would be. I am helpless there."

"So am I. I am not fitted for an ordinary domestic life."

"So I must live with someone who is. And I shall not see the life as ordinary. None is so to me."

"How do you see your own life? It is even less so to you?"

"It is as it is. As I am what I am. I know I am a man of full nature. I know I am built on a large scale. I am not afraid to say it."

"It is true that most people would be. If I thought it of myself, I should. So you can't know if I think it. But do you know anyone who thinks he is built on a small scale?"

"I know many people who are. It is part of their interest to me."

"But not of their interest to themselves. Do they know on what scale they are?"

"I am to marry someone who is on a moderate one, and who knows it."

"Then I guess who it is. There is someone of whom it is true. And there would not be anyone else."

6

"My father perhaps?"

"But you can hardly marry him, Hereward."

"In effect I have done so. We are all wedded to each other. My wife must fit into a human framework. It is a demand I have to make."

"And you feel you can make it. You know the woman who is to meet it. You are not in doubt."

"I am not. I have my own knowledge of Ada Merton. Her qualities are many. I would not marry a woman I could not depend on and trust. I know I have had my early time. But in her own way she has had hers."

"Well, there is the attraction of opposites. Though I never quite believe in it. It is safer to depend on qualities held in common. What will your parents feel about your marriage?"

"They will be glad to hear of it. They will welcome the thought of grandchildren. It is the natural, usual thing."

"What of your sister? There is the touchstone. I will not speak of her scale. We do not question it."

"She has always helped me. She will help me now. I have imagined her as your sister. I thought she would be."

"But then I should be a sister too. And I have not a sister's qualities. I don't even know what they are. No doubt you can tell me."

"I can, and they are great ones. I have seen some of them in you."

"If you and I were married, think of the scale of our children! With both of us on such a considerable one. A house with such a brood! It could not stand."

"It would have stood. But it was not to be. I wonder if you will regret it. People may see you as a disappointed woman."

"They will. And I shall wish they knew I was not. I may be on a small scale after all."

"You may be, Rosa. You are," said Hereward with

sudden force. "You are content with too little. My wife will have more than you. To have a thing we must accept it. You could be the first person in my life. You choose to be nothing, and it is what you will be. I cannot play a double part."

"Not with me. But I should have thought you could. I fear you will, and I think you fear it. I know you, and you know yourself."

"I do. I wish I did not. I know the forces within me. I know they may rise up at any time. As you have found, they have sometimes risen. I don't exhaust them on my work. They are not easily spent. The effort seems to give them strength, to set them free. You have been my safeguard. You could always be."

"No, the forces would be there. You are not for the single path."

"Rosa, I shall be a good husband."

"You may be what you mean by the words."

"I will see that Ada finds me what she should."

"In time she must find what you are. There is no escape."

"Do I not offer a good deal?"

"What do you ask? Your home is your father's. She will not be its mistress."

"I did not know you considered such things."

"I may not. We are not talking of me."

"She is a good daughter and sister. She does not ask much for herself."

"But now she may ask more. Will she marry to have the same?"

"She will have what I give her," said Hereward, again with force. "She will take it and be content. What is the good of your rejecting me yourself, and bringing all this against my marrying someone else? You know the way to prevent it."

"There is nothing against your marrying her. There is everything in its favour. I was saying what there was against her marrying you. Does she know what it is?"

"She knows nothing. She will know nothing. And there may be nothing to know."

"Let there be nothing, Hereward. Let there always be nothing. It will help you both. And there are many of you, and there may be more. It will help you all."

CHAPTER II

"My wife, there may be trouble coming. We will meet it with a brave heart. We have faced too much together to fail in these our latter days."

"What have we faced, Michael? I don't think I can remember anything."

"Ah, Joanna, our home is in danger. This old roof over our heads. It has sheltered our fathers, and may not pass to our son. Hand-in-hand we came in, in our youth and hope. Hand-in-hand we would go out, depending on each other, and the knowledge that we had harmed no one. Ah, no one is the worse for our downfall. That must be our stay. Without it we were poor indeed."

"It sounds as if we should be poor with it. And some people must be the worse, if you mean we are in debt."

"Ah, debt presses on us, Joanna. And the creditors have no pity. The old words mean nothing to them: 'Blessed are the merciful'. But our courage will not fail us. If our home passes to other hands, we will witness it, dumb and dry-eyed. If strangers cast on it appraising eyes and utter belittling words, we will stand aside and be silent."

"Are they really as bad as that? When the house was in danger before, they said such nice things about it. And about what they would make of it, when it was theirs. I hardly knew its possibilities. I was quite sorry they could not have it."

"Well, I was not," said Sir Michael Egerton. "I was glad we could keep it. Because what would happen to us without it I am at a loss to say. It would be the end of our world."

The old house in question was large and beautiful and

shabby, but only the last to any unusual degree. It had the appeal of a place where lack of means had prevented the addition of new things, and ensured care of the old. The land about it stretched to a fair distance, and in the past had provided its support.

"The end of the world never comes. And there are always people who expect it."

"Well, it may not come, my wife. Matters may adjust themselves. They have done so before."

"I don't think they have. It has had to be done for them. It will be done for them again. I can't say that Hereward will do it. It might seem that I was taking it as a matter of course."

"I hope we are not, Joanna. I hope we have not sunk so far. What would you say, Galleon? I know you have not missed a word."

"Well, Sir Michael," said the butler, who had not done so, "would it not be giving credit where credit is due?"

"Rendering to Caesar the things that are Caesar's. Well, I suppose it would. It has come to be our part."

"And it must be nice to be Caesar," said Joanna. "I think Hereward must like it. I am sure I should."

"Ah, Joanna, I am forced to lean where once I led. It goes against the grain. It would be at once better and worse to have no dear ones."

"For us it would be worse. I don't know what to say about them. I suppose we are their dear ones. We have to assume we are. Well, they say that all love has its sad side."

"Ah, ha, well, I suppose it has. We are looking to them, I admit. Well, we must be worthy of them. We must not bring faint hearts to the stress of life. We must face our indebtedness, shoulder the burden and carry it with us. We will not bend beneath it, heavy in its way though it be. Is not that our own victory?"

"Yes, it is. We can be sure it would not be anyone else's."

"What would you call it, Galleon?"

"I can hardly say, Sir Michael."

"Ah, the humble part is the hard one. Gratitude is the rare thing to give. In a sense it is a gift. If we can give it, nothing is beyond us. To render it is the way to be unvanquished by it."

"It must be difficult to be vanquished," said Joanna. "I hardly see how anyone could be."

"Ah, you can smile to yourself, Galleon. That is always your line. You don't know the cost of some of the stresses of life. I can only think you have escaped them."

"These would hardly arise in my situation, Sir Michael."

"They come from things that are common to us all."

"It is the degree in which those are held, that is not common to us, Sir Michael. But I have no claim to them. It falls to me to observe them in other hands. And I think there may be news of some of them. The post is here, and, if I am right, a lawyer's letter. I am familiar with their aspect."

"Yes, no doubt you are. And so am I. I am sure I wish I was not. You are right. I wish you were wrong. It is a lawyer's letter. And from Messrs Blount and Middleman, names that strike a chill to my soul. Middleman! It is the right word. Something between ourselves and human good. Now what a profession to choose! One that brings trouble and anxiety to innocent people. And does little else as far as I can see. Except cause threats and mysteries where there is none. It must be an odd man who wants it. I would rather bring a little peace and goodwill myself. Well, Messrs Blount and Middleman, and what have you to say? Is it my fault that tithes and rents fall, and expenses rise? What have I done to cause it? Nothing but lead a simple life and harm no one. Well, let us read your letter. The courage it needs! I declare I am without it. Strong man that I am, I have not enough to open it."

"Perhaps her ladyship could be of help to you, Sir Michael."

"No, she could not. I should not ask it of her. I am not a man who talks about the courage of women. It is for a man to show courage himself. So here is the moment. My Joanna, be prepared. It is the last straw that may break us. But we will show our mettle. We come of stock that has it. Come here and read it with me. I can't put a hand on my glasses."

"Your hand happens to be on them, Sir Michael."

"Yes, so it does. So I can read it myself. And I don't care what it is. It cannot be laid to my account.—So the land by the river is sold. The piece that has been on the market. The figures of the sale are here. And the expenses and the agent's commission. They would not be left out. Come and look at them, Joanna. Figures are out of my line. I have come to be afraid of them. Messrs Blount and the other have frightened me. I shudder at the thought of them.—What? Is that what it is? Money and a real sum of it! Enough to mean something! I don't know how to believe it. I will not believe it for the time. I will let it soak in. I will savour it. I will have some moments of relief. They do not come too often. Well, if money is the root of all evil, it is the root of other things too. There is no evil here that I can see. This delivers us, Joanna. This opens up our path. Forward can be our watchword. Forward, with heads up, eyes on the future, strong in heart."

"If I may say so, Sir Michael, the money is capital, and should be seen and used as such."

"Well, you may not say so. Who do you think you are? Messrs Blount and Middleman? One example of them is enough. A douche of cold water is not what we want at the moment. You should know that at your age. A man of forty should be equal to it. And money is money, capital or not. You can't get away from it."

"Is capital exactly money?" said Joanna. "If it was, it could be spent. It is a large amount, that brings in small ones without getting any less. And the small ones are spent; and their being so small leads people into debt. But it seems kind and clever of capital. We should not ask any more."

"True, my lady," said Galleon. "We must not kill the thing we love."

"Do I love capital? I suppose I do. It is dreadful to love money. I did not know I did. But capital is so kind to us. I am sure anyone would love it. And it is sad if it is sometimes killed. It makes me love it more."

"Well, what I love is a little ease," said Sir Michael, leaning back as if to enjoy it. "I am a man of sixty, and it is time I had it. And I want it for you as much as for myself. More, of course; I want it chiefly for you. And for all the people in whose debt we are. Ah, I have thought of them, Joanna. My mind has not been only on myself. I have pictured them in want of what was theirs. I have not been blind to their claims. Because what is owed to them is theirs in a way. I have recognised it."

"They have recognised it too. You and they seem to be alike. But it seems somehow inconsistent of them. Thinking it is theirs, when it is spent! They seem to love money as much as I do. And not to be ashamed of it. It makes me quite ashamed for them. They might have behaved nobly, and they have not."

"Ah, we do not meet that, Joanna. We must not look for it, my wife. Self is what it is in their minds, self and little else. But they have been in mine. In it and on it, day and night. Sleeping and waking, I have had them in my thought. I have had to hold myself from dwelling on them. It was all I could do."

"Well, if you did all you could! It is known that no one can do more."

"Well, it is in the past. Our way is clear. My heart sings at the thought. It leaps for them and for ourselves. Let us celebrate it, Joanna. This renews the days when our yoke was easy and our burden light."

The pair moved together and executed movements

14

reminiscent of these days, while Galleon's large, pale eyes surveyed them from his large, pale face, his large, pale, skilful hands perhaps more usefully employed.

Sir Michael and his wife were both grey-haired and dark-eyed, tall and upright and active for their age. They were distant cousins, and a likeness was sometimes discerned in them. Sir Michael's broad features had a look of having failed to mature, while Joanna's, of similar type, were strongly formed and marked with lines of mirth. His hands, inert and solid and somehow kind, seemed a part of himself; and hers, spare and active and also kind, had a life of their own. Their common age of sixty was acknowledged by Joanna openly, and would not have been owned by Sir Michael at all, if his wife could have been depended on.

"Well, here is a scene," said their daughter's voice. "Shall we find ourselves equal to it? We have put away childish things."

"Come, it is too soon for such a pose. Come and join your mother and me. Try to be as young as we are. We are celebrating good news. Good for ourselves and others; that is the happy part. Joy for ourselves is not true joy for us. This is the real thing."

"Say what has happened," said Zillah to her mother, as though taking the shortest line to the truth.

"Some money has fallen in. Some land is sold. We could pay what we owe, if the money was not capital. Or if capital was money, as your father thinks it is. He feels so kindly to creditors. And people so seldom do. I never speak of them myself. It might sound as if we were in debt."

Zillah Egerton was shorter than her mother, and seemed to be darker, as she was not grey-haired. She had Joanna's definite features, but not Sir Michael's look of ease. She gave an impression of controlled energy, as Hereward gave one of effort to keep his under control. The gravity and perception of her face seemed the complement of the force in his. At thirty-two and thirty-four they had the air and poise of middle age.

"The land by the river!" said Hereward, guided to the letter by a sign from Galleon. "Of course the money is capital. It must be invested. It is an appreciable part of the estate. Debts must be paid out of income. They were contracted in the ordinary course. They would be incurred again, if this method of payment were followed. You suggested that we should be as young as you are. It is a good thing we are not."

"Now come, think again," said Sir Michael. "Let your thought go below the surface; let it go a little deep, pass beyond ourselves. The money is not ours to invest. Others have the prior claim. Money that is owed belongs to the people it is owed to. We must be just to them, before we are generous to ourselves and our own ideas."

"Papa, you deceive no one," said Zillah. "I suppose you don't really deceive yourself."

"I really try to," said Joanna. "I don't understand money matters, and I keep my eyes from them, in case they are really easy to understand. It is best not to listen to Hereward, when clever people make everything clear in a few words."

"I hardly seem to do so," said her son. "But I must ask my father to hear me. He cannot keep his eyes from the truth. I have no choice but to force it upon him. He is not a woman."

"Force it upon me! There is a way to talk. Am I or am I not your father? And not a woman! Why should I be one? Are you a woman yourself?"

"Neither of us is a child. And you are not an old man. You may have a future before you. And you are on a road that has no turning. You must simply retrace your steps."

"I will have no trouble for your mother," said Sir Michael, in a warning tone. "If anything you mean involves that, leave it unsaid. If other people suffer, she suffers with them. That is a thing I will not have, and there is an end of it."

"There is an end of it all," said Hereward, after a pause. "There need have been no beginning. I will not waste my words. It is a waste of what is behind them, and that would mean another end. I will let you have the money, and replace it from what I earn. I can't see the place bled to death."

"Well, no, we can't. I feel it as much as you do. There is the future to consider. We have to think of other lives. There may be descendants in the end. Of course we feel there will be. You are a good son, Hereward. We have reason to be grateful to you. We are not afraid of the word."

"It is the natural one," said Zillah. "I wonder if you know how little you should be afraid of it."

"I don't dare to know," said Joanna. "I shut my eyes to the truth. It does seem that we are eating our cake and having it. And I should have thought we were, if it was not known to be impossible."

"It is, unless someone supplies another cake."

"Yes, well, that is true," said Sir Michael, on a rueful note. "Yes, well, that is what it is. And we must be thankful for it. And thankful that the money comes in. It is strange that it should come just from writing books like novels. It seems such a light sort of thing. But of course people do earn by it, even more than by serious books they say. Well, if it is so, we are the better for it."

"It is one of the most exacting of the arts," said Zillah. "Few people can go far in it."

"Is it? Is that so? Well, you know best. But I always feel I could write a novel, if I tried. But I am a bad person for trying, and that is the truth."

"You may be a bad person for achieving. Anyone can try."

"Is that really true?" said Joanna. "Could we all settle down and make an effort? Then I will just forget it."

"Well, so will I," said her husband. "I don't know

what I could have done, if I had been able for that. I often feel possibilities welling up within me. But it is late for them to get out. The time is past."

"You are both talking of what you don't understand."

"Well, otherwise should we not talk too little?" said Joanna. "And not to either of you at all?"

"Well, I think I can understand a novel," said Sir Michael. "It would be odd if I couldn't manage that. It is not as if it had thought or learning in it. It is just about ordinary experiences that anyone might have. There is no question of not understanding."

"They are imaginary," said Zillah. "And imagination is the highest kind of thought."

"Well, writers must imagine something, if they haven't any knowledge. They must put something into a book. And they put in actual events and people; even the great ones; it seems to be accepted. I never know why they are great myself. It seems an easy thing to do. And it can't be called imagination, whatever kind of thought it is."

"We can mistake Hereward's silence. It is his way of being patient," said Zillah, showing she had found no way herself.

"Patient, is he? Well, I think other people have to be that. Why, he can't be approached about anything, and is put out, if his door is opened twice in a day. He can't have a room without a door, and it has to be put to its natural use. He says it drives things out of his head. But he can think of something else. It can't be so hard, or he could not write all those books. Long ones too; I give him credit there. The mere writing must be a task, even if there isn't much more to it. But I wonder he did not work on a man's line, while he was about it."

"What do you do on what you call a man's line yourself?"

"Now that shows how much you know about my life. Problems arise, and questions are asked, and complaints pour in. And can I say a word to Hereward about the place that will be his? No, I must wait until he emerges, dazed and dumb and vacant-eyed. I should like to tell him to wake up sometimes. And I would, if I dared."

"No one should dare to tell anyone that," said Joanna. "It is too simple to have so much courage."

"Well, I haven't it. So you need not fear. I am quite without it. If a father can be afraid of his son, that father is before you."

"Hereward is absorbed in the lives he imagines," said Zillah. "He can't be so alert to this one."

"Is he? Is that what it is? Well, things are not what they seem. Of course we know they are not. It has become a saying. Well, I am blind to it all. He has chosen a line apart from me."

"And one more apart than you know. One where many are called, but few chosen."

"Well, put like that, I have no choice but to accept it. If that is so, it is. So Hereward is one by himself. Well, of course we know he is. And we look up to him. We are grateful to him. We realise where we should be without him. We are thankful for every word that falls from his pen. And other people are grateful too. Look at the things that are said of him. Why, my heart swells with pride. Tears come into my eyes, and I am not ashamed of it. I quite tremble to think I am his father."

"I expect he trembles at it too," said Joanna. "But people are always ashamed of their parents. So it hardly matters if they are more ashamed than usual."

"Ashamed of us, are they? Well, it is a feeling I don't return. I am proud of them. Proud of my son for what he achieves, and of my daughter for the help she gives him. I look up to my children. And if they look down on us, well, it can happen, as you say. And they have a right to look down on us. We are not equal to them. I mean, of course, that I am not. No man would look down on his mother. It need not be said."

"Only part of my work is of use to you," said

Hereward. "It is the part that should not mean the most to me."

"Well, it means it to me. I should be ungrateful if it did not. Why, it is the part that gives us something. I don't see much point in work for its own sake. It is an odd, conceited view. And it is a wrong kind of conceit. The labourer is worthy of his hire. That would not be stated where it is, if it was not true."

"My books are read for different reasons. We should be willing to write for the few."

"Well, I am glad you write for the many too. It is natural that I should be. I am one of the many myself. And it gives the whole thing its meaning. The few have too much done for them. To serve the many is a larger aim. And it is best from your own point of view. Why should you toil and get nothing out of it? Or nothing in your own time. I often wonder how poets and painters feel, if they know about things in an after life. And novelists too. They are artists too in a way. Oh, I think about these things more than you know."

"I am sure Hereward did not know," said Joanna. "I believe I hardly knew myself. I am proud of you, Michael. And I see that our children must be more and more ashamed."

"Well, I talk and think in my own way. We all have our ways of doing everything. And of course mine is not theirs. I often wonder how my children came about. It escapes me. I can't explain it."

"Something may have come to them through me. Not from me. It has passed me over."

"Yes, it has missed a generation. That is a thing that does happen. I know there were unusual people in your family, and that they had no recognition in their time. It rather bears out what I have said. Well, Galleon, and what do you say to my son's manner of life? What is your opinion of it?"

"Well, Sir Michael, if there happens to be necessity, it

does not involve anything manual," said Galleon, making this clear.

"Well, I am not so sure. Scratching and scribbling and shuffling papers! It does that into the bargain."

"Well, not to the point of soiling the hands, Sir Michael."

"The ink and dust are equal to it, I should think."

"Well, they may have their own suggestion, Sir Michael."

"Would you like to write a book, Galleon?"

"Well, I have often thought of it, Sir Michael. The simplicity of it is before one's eyes, as it might seem."

"Yes, it puts it into people's heads. I wonder I have never set my hand to it. It is a thing I shall never explain."

"No doubt there is explanation in both cases, Sir Michael."

"You mean you have not the time, and I have not the talent? Ah, I can read your thought, Galleon. I can often read people's minds. That might be useful to me, if I wrote. But the time is past. And one writer in a house is enough."

"And the other pursuits are necessary, Sir Michael. To enable the writing to take place and the results to ensue."

"Ah, you are indispensable, Galleon. Mr. Hereward's work depends on yours, and so we all depend on it," said Sir Michael, again using his gift of reading minds. "Ah, we give you your due. Yes, you can go to your work, and so can he. Yes, your sister will go with you, Hereward. Ah, you have a helpmate in my Zillah. You have your comrade there. And I am glad to know it. It is a solace to me. I don't always feel you have sympathy in your home. I sometimes think we fail you there. And you do not fail us. You don't indeed. You have lifted a weight from us to-day. We respect work that does so much for us. If we have given another impression, it is a wrong one. My Joanna, our future is safe. We need not hide our joy. Galleon, can you imagine our son and daughter celebrating matters in this way?"

"It may not need such a feat of imagination, Sir Michael," said Galleon, who knew that the pair in question were indulging in mimicry of the activity, as they went upstairs.

"Which of our parents is the greater character?" said Zillah, when they reached her brother's room.

"Pappa. Mamma is the greater person. How you protect me from them! From those arch enemies of the artist, parents and home. Where should I be without you? Where should any of us be?"

"So many of your readers must be parents, and more must live in a home. It is no wonder that your best work is too little known."

"Ah, Zillah, I am content. All my work is my own. If I serve many thousands of people I am glad to know I serve them. It is no ignoble task. What comes from my brain comes from myself, and I would not disown it. My best work, as it is called, is no more deeply mine. And its serving fewer gives it no higher place. Everything springs from the same source. I feel it is the same. But we can't control our brains as we control our movements. When I am in the power of mine, I don't belong to myself. Well, you will be on guard to-day. No one must come to my door. Meals can be sent up, if there is need."

The need arose, and Sir Michael heard the order given. "So the force is at work," he said, as he came to the luncheon table. "But it must need fuel like anything else. And that could be supplied down here."

"It breaks a train of thought to take part in ordinary talk," said Zillah.

"Hereward does not take part in it. He sits like a stork with his mind elsewhere. And eats as if he was doing something else, as I suppose he is. But he has a life apart from his thought. He can't feed himself with a pen. And we must use a knife and fork, as he does. I don't see there is all that difference. You will say that he feeds us all with his pen. Ah, ha, I forestalled you there. I took the words out of your mouth. There is not such a gulf between us."

"It is natural that the words should be in our mouths. The thought must be in our minds."

"Well, well, it is in yours, I know. It may be too seldom in mine. But it does not lessen my pride in my son. Why, I read things about him that quite take me aback. And I say to myself: 'I am the father of this man. I gave him life. Whatever he has done, I have done myself in a way.' It is a serious thought. I am sobered by it."

"You knew not what you did," said his daughter.

"Well, no, it is true in a sense. And yet it is not, you know. Why, sometimes I understand him as well as anyone. Parts of his books have brought tears to my eyes. And I have not been ashamed of it. And I have laughed too. Why, I have thrown back my head and laughed until tears came of another kind, and I was quite glad no one was there to witness it. I have been lost to anything outside myself. I don't deny it."

"That was when anyone might have witnessed it."

"Oh, well, was it? So the funny parts are the best. Well, I should hardly have thought it. They seem more on anyone's level. And yet I am not sure, you know. I sometimes see light on things in a way. I might make more of myself, if I tried."

"People would not like you to try," said Joanna. "They think we make enough of ourselves. And they would see you trying and despise you."

"Well, I should not care if they did. I don't always think as much of them as they believe. Why, when Hereward and Zillah talk, I often glimpse their hidden meanings, though I don't try to get the credit. It is as I have said. Indolence is my trouble. I might have been a different man without it."

"We should all be different without our distinguishing

qualities," said Zillah. "Not that our meanings are probably so deeply hidden."

"Well, not from your father. There are games that two can play at. It does not do to forget it."

"They are a good son and daughter," said Joanna. "We would not have them changed. Ought not one of us to say it?"

"Joanna, if I saw a hint of change in either of them, I should be distressed. It would be a grief to me. I would not alter one jot or one tittle of their qualities. I am not equal to them. I look up to them. My heart swells at the thought of them. They are superior to their father. If ever a man was thankful for his wife and children, I am that man. Well, Galleon, do you not feel I do well to be thankful?"

"No one could take exception to the feeling, Sir Michael."

"I daresay you could see some cause for discontent."

"No real one, Sir Michael. There are perhaps circumstances that might be found unexpected."

"My son's doing work that you find so? You feel we should be mildly ashamed of it?"

"I should not use that word, Sir Michael. I see no disgrace in honest work. I need only adduce my own case. But in some we may look for a difference."

"And you don't see it in this one? Well, I am a proud father, whether you believe it or not."

"There seems no room for doubt of it, Sir Michael."

"But you would not be proud in my place?"

"It is the place that might prevent it, Sir Michael."

"Galleon, my son is a household word."

"I have gathered that that is the position, Sir Michael."

"And you hardly like to refer to it?"

"I do not often find it necessary, Sir Michael."

"You would not betray us, unless you were obliged to?"

"I respect any private circumstance in the family, Sir Michael."

"This has surely become public."

"It could hardly fail to in the end, Sir Michael."

"So it would be no good to deny it."

"It is hardly a case for actual suppression, Sir Michael," said Galleon, as he moved away.

"Ah, Joanna, 'a prophet is not without honour'. We can see that Hereward has too little in his home. I caught a glimpse of myself in Galleon. And I felt ashamed and resolved to do better."

"He sees the disgrace in honest work, though he had to deny it. And how did the saying arise, if no one saw it? And how can it be seen, if it is not there? I wonder if I could see it, if I dared."

"Well, I cannot and will not see it. If I were not proud and grateful, I should be less than a man. And I wish I did some honest work myself. I have come to wish it. I should be glad to be of help to someone. I envy Galleon, and he can hear me say it. Do you hear me, Galleon? I envy you for doing useful work in the world."

"Work can only be done in the world, Sir Michael. There is no other locality for it. And you would envy a good many people, the larger number. Myself among them, as you say."

"I see you don't believe me."

"I know you believe yourself at the moment, Sir Michael."

"Do you ever envy anyone?"

"Envy is one of the seven deadly sins, Sir Michael," said Galleon with a smile. "I hope I should not yield to it."

"Do you like to be envied yourself?"

"I might like a position that involved it, Sir Michael. It has not fallen to me. I have remained below it."

"I have always felt that people below me must envy me," said Joanna, in an undertone. "Of course I know they are not below. I wonder who ever thought they were. Again I think someone must have."

"Do you take any interest in our actual life?" said

Zillah, as though her own interest in the other matters had failed.

"Oh, in Hereward's marriage?" said her father. "The hint of it has come before and meant nothing. And now there is no word of the woman. He can't be married without a wife, any more than the rest of us."

"That is true. It is why it will make a difference."

"Ah, it would to you, my poor girl. Your father knows it would. You would be the first to suffer."

"Or the last," said Joanna. "Or the one not to suffer at all. Hereward will marry without a wife as far as anyone can."

"Well, I hope he will marry in one way or another. It would be a step forward for him and all of us. I should welcome his wife as a daughter. I should rejoice in his fulfilment. I have not got so little out of marriage myself, that I should regret it for my son. And it would be good to have descendants, Joanna, to have our own kind of immortality. I know you think we have no other. I leave the question myself as something beyond me."

"I should be glad to have the descendants. I don't mind about the immortality. It is not of a kind that matters."

"Well, well, the generations pass. We have to play our part. What do you feel about these questions, Galleon? Do you ever wish you were a married man?"

"Well, I see there is something to be said for it, Sir Michael. Perhaps more on the other side."

"You would not like to have descendants?"

"I hardly know what they would do for me, Sir Michael. And I should have to do much for them. More than my resources warranted."

"Why, they would grow up and work for you, Galleon."

"They would grow up at my expense and work for themselves, Sir Michael. There would be no alternative. And so it would go on."

"To think that we are all descendants!" said Joanna.

"I am sure I am above the average. I have never worked for myself. It does sound egotistic."

"Well, I have worked for myself and others in managing things," said Sir Michael. "I think it is a just claim."

"Yes, Sir Michael. Though most work is for others," said Galleon, leaving the matter there.

"I think all claims are just," said Joanna. "That is why they are made. I have never met an unjust claim. I suppose it is because there are not any."

CHAPTER III

"Now would Aunt Penelope approve of this idleness, Emmeline?"

"No. Nor approve of anything. She cannot feel approval."

"She wants you to get on. She is thinking of your future. With such neighbours as the Egertons we must keep our wits alive. Or we shall not hold our own with them."

"I don't know what my own is. And it is better not to know. Then I shall not have to come into it."

"You know Father wants you to be educated."

"But then I should be different. And he seems to like me as I am."

"So do we all. We don't want our little one altered. We want her to grow into her full self."

"I believe I am that already. But it is best for people not to know it. They think more of me."

"Oh, I can't think what to say to you. You must be a changeling. And you will have to live in the world, like everyone else."

"No, not like everyone. Only like myself. That is all I shall try to do."

"It may not be so easy. You won't always be sixteen."

"I feel as if I should. And I think in a way I shall."

"I am sometimes afraid you will."

"You set me a good example. You won't always be twenty-five. You have already ceased to be it."

"I forgot my age when Mother died. It was the only thing, if I was to remember yours. Oh, I know Aunt Penelope came to take her place. And has done so with Father, as far as it could be done. But it ended there,

28

and other things devolved on me. Oh, I don't mean I am not grateful to her. She takes Father off my mind. She does for him what I could not do. He does not see me as on his mental level. How can he, when I am not? We must be content to be ourselves. I did hope to be his right hand in other ways, and to be seen by him as such. But it was not to be. Aunt Penelope loomed too large. Not of set purpose; as the result of the difference between us. I am the first person to recognise it. Though Father's recognising it so soon made me a thought rueful I admit."

"It was Aunt Penelope who recognised it. He never thinks of the difference between her and me."

"He does not, you fortunate elf. The difference is too great. So in a sense it might not be there. But I was a step on the way. I tried and failed. I aspired to be what I was not. And so I remained what I am."

"Aunt Penelope says I should improve myself. All she sees in me is room for improvement."

"She is not quite right there. And I confess I don't mind her being a little wrong sometimes."

"She and Father are not alike, are they?"

"Heaven forbid!" said Ada, lifting her hands. "If there is a more disparate brother and sister, I have yet to meet them. But she serves Father's purpose. And so serves ours in a way. She may have saved us from a stepmother. So I am grateful to her, or feel I should be, which is much the same thing."

"I think it is quite different."

"So it is, you perceptive sprite. I was making a false claim. I can't go the whole length with her, and that is the truth. I see her qualities; I see the scale she is built on; I recognise my second place. But I can't whole-heartedly go the full way. It is a thing I can't explain."

"I think you have explained it."

"So I have. And I have explained myself as well. And a poor figure I cut, in my own estimation anyhow. I hope it is disguised from other people. I think I have a right to that. For it is not my true level. I shall rise above it. I am determined, and that is half the battle. I will not lose hold of myself."

"A strong resolve," said a resonant voice, as Miss Merton entered the room, a tall, spare, elderly woman, with an experienced expression, resigned, grey eyes and an untypical but definite face. "But one we can keep, if we will. We have ourselves in our own hands."

"So we have, Aunt Penelope. And it is a power I am resolved to use. It does not matter along what line. We need not pursue it."

"We will not, as we are not invited to," said her aunt, smiling. "Our dealings with ourselves are our own."

"Is Father in his study? Is he happy by himself? I thought he seemed harassed at breakfast."

"That was natural, as he was harassed. He is at the end of some work, and beset by the final troubles."

"I wish I could be of some help. How impotent I feel!"

"You wish you were older and more erudite. It is natural that you are not."

"I don't wish she was either," said Emmeline.

"No, I wish I had the nameless thing that you have, Aunt Penelope. I don't think it depends on age and erudition. Those might come to me in the end; and one of them must come; but that will not. I am in no doubt about it. And neither are you."

Miss Penelope smiled again on her brother's girls, her expression suggesting that she accepted them as they were. Ada was tall and strong and upright, with an opaque, clear skin, thick, brown hair, slightly puzzled, blue eyes and features that were pleasant and plain. Her sister was short and plump and fair, with a pale, full face and uneven, childish features that somehow attained the point of charm. She suggested the confidence in her own appeal, that her family accepted and encouraged.

The house they lived in was book-lined and not without grace, and seemed like a home from an old university moved to the country, which in its essence and life it was.

"Well, is my pupil prepared for me? I have given her time."

"I fear she is not," said Ada. "And I fear the fault is mine. Other subjects arose, and I admit I myself was one of them."

"Well, they may have had their claim. Certainly the last one had."

"A little learning is a dangerous thing," said Emmeline. "And I should never have much. So perhaps I am better without it."

"Better than many of us, I believe," said her aunt, smiling.

"You are right, Aunt Penelope," said Ada. "It is large of you to see it. Ah, the old sayings are the best. Their wisdom never wears out. 'A little learning' and the rest. 'He does much who does a little well'. They hold the truth."

"Perhaps the surface of it. I think not always more. When someone does a little well, that is what he does. And very little it can be. Is there more truth in the theory of the great failure?"

"There may be. And perhaps a little truth in that of the small one. I must hope there is, as that is what I shall be. I feel it more when I talk to you, and glimpse the something beyond myself. But I remain an advocate of sayings. They give us wisdom in a nutshell. And that is what we need."

"There can't be room for much in one," said Emmeline.

"I think there is not," said her aunt. "Real knowledge must have depth and scope. I say nothing for the condensed or more likely the reduced form of it."

"Well, it is better than nothing," said Ada. "Though again I glimpse the gulf between us. Half a loaf may be better than no bread."

"Half is a good deal," said Emmeline. "And is it much good for a thing to be great, when it is failure?"

31

"Well, what is the talk?" said a deep voice, as Penelope's brother entered the room, a tall, handsome, grey-haired man, whose features suggested his sister's controlled to a better form. "Let me know the matter in hand."

"The great failure, Father," said Ada. "Aunt Penelope pleads ably for it. I was content to take a humbler stand."

"If by great, you mean on a considerable scale, I would hardly plead for it. I am involved in one."

"Oh, no, you are not, Father. It is the exhaustion after a prolonged effort. You need not fear. I do not for you."

"I share people's fears for themselves," said Penelope. "They have the true basis."

"But we need not encourage them. We can render a better service. I do feel my line is right there."

"Mr. and Miss Egerton," said a servant at the door.

"Now you have come at an opportune moment," said Ada. "You find my father out of heart, and can say a word to cheer him. You can be no strangers to the reaction after endeavour. You have a twofold knowledge of it, as your two lives are one."

"It is true," said Hereward. "But reaction may not come by itself. It tends to carry a sense of unsuccess. You are right that I am no stranger to it. I can offer nothing better than sympathy."

"But that may be the best thing. To feel that some-one suffers what you do, that it is not an isolated experience, may lift the heart more than anything. You may have said the word that was needed. I somehow felt you would."

"We are helped in trouble by knowing we are not alone in it," said Penelope, with a note of condoning the truth.

"Yes, Aunt Penelope. If either was flushed with success, the other might feel the contrast, would be bound to feel it. As it is, each is uplifted. I am sure I am right."

"You may be," said Zillah. "It does sound like knowledge of our nature."

32

"Well, that is a thing I have. It is a fair claim. It is my own peculiar province, natural to me. It comes to me not out of books, but from something in myself. Human life goes on all round me; human nature is emplified in it. I have watched it and drawn my own conclusions, weighed them in the balance and not found them wanting. I am a companion for anyone on that ground."

"Then will you be my companion, Ada?" said Hereward, moving towards her. "My province is the same as yours. We need the same companionship. My sister and I have it, and would give it to you. And be grateful if you would take and return it."

There was the moment of silence. Ada's father came to her side. She was the first to find her words.

"Why, I did not know that proposals took place in public like this."

"They do not. This is not a usual one," said Hereward. "It offers what is usual, but it asks more. You would share a home with my parents and my sister. Share me with her, and give her a part of yourself. You see why I make it in your father's hearing. It seemed that he should know the whole."

"Dear Sir Michael and Lady Egerton! It would be a privilege to share a home with them. And I have always wanted Zillah's friendship, and felt it was presumptuous of me. There is only advantage for me there."

"Then if you will share even more with me, and share it always, may I feel our word is pledged?" said Hereward, taking her hand and looking at Alfred.

"Yes, there is something to be done there. My father's consent must be sought and gained before we go any further. Father, you have no objection to Hereward as a son?"

"None to him as a son. As my daughter's husband it is hard to be sure. He asks, as he says, more than other men. Is he to give any more? You have a stable nature;

I have valued it, my dear. He is more uncertain, and, as I should judge, could be carried away. If there are risks in the future, are they his or yours?"

"They are mine, Father. I face them with open eyes. I am prepared to give some quarter. I don't feel I am so much in myself. I am hardly on the level of Hereward and Zillah, and am not unwilling to redress the balance."

"As your father I can hardly support that account."

"Nor can I," said Hereward. "I accept it even less than you. I don't ask you to trust me with your daughter. That is asking much. If she will trust herself to me, I will accept and fulfil the trust. I think it is for her to judge."

"I have judged, Father," said Ada.

"Then I have no more to say. But I have meant what I said. I hope you will never have to remember my saying it. Well, so the change is to come. And I am not to lose my daughter. And to welcome the son I have not had. I can say with Ada that there is only advantage for me there."

"You are to have more than a son, Father. You will have a fellow-worker. There will be a healthy rivalry. The scholar and the novelist pitted against each other. With me as the intermediary, ensuring that it remains healthy. Well, it is a character I can fill. It is the sort of secondary one that fits me. Indeed all the parts I am to play will be suited to myself. I need feel no qualm."

"How you think of yourself, Hereward!" said Emmeline. "You forget that Ada has a sister. She does not like you any better than me, and you will not have the whole of her. I shall often be with her, whether you want me or not."

"And with me too, Emmeline," said Hereward, drawing her to him. "You will be with both of us. I shall be your brother. Don't you know that is part of it to me?"

"Oh, what a sister to have!" said Ada. "If our places were reversed, should I have had this welcome? I doubt it. Indeed, I can imagine the difference. It may be a salutary exercise for me. Oh, I expect you will have little interchanges of your own. Well, I will not grudge them to you."

"Then you and I will have them," said Zillah. "We will have as many, and they will both grudge them."

"Ah, the kind of word I was waiting for! I hesitated to say it myself, in case it should not come first from me. But coming from you, it is the very one for me. I am the last person to put the man before the woman. I am a staunch upholder of my own sex. You may not be sure if I justify my own opinion. In the case of this little sprite there will be no doubt."

"It is the life before you and me, that is in my mind, Ada," said Hereward. "And I hope in yours."

"Yes, it is in mine. Too deep down to take form in words. Not that we can enter on it on quite equal terms. That is a thing that cannot be. Mine is an open sheet, with everything written on it plainly for your eyes. Yours will have its spaces and erasures. A man's life is not a woman's. I am not a woman to expect it. Oh, they are metaphorical sheets, little Emmeline, but none the less real for that. As you will understand, when you have things written on your own. At present it must be a blank."

"She and I will write on it," said Hereward, smiling. "We shall find our words."

"Oh, I expect you will," said Ada, with a sigh. "I shall be out of it sometimes. I am prepared. It is no new thing. She and Father indulge in companionship that I do not share. I have learned to accept it."

"I scarcely knew it," said Alfred. "And she and Hereward will not. The companionship will be between you and him."

"Yes, in another sense, Father. As it has been between you and me. Oh, I have understood. I have been content with my place. It is a content that is natural to me. I am even content with my own face, with the example of yours before me. And when mine should resemble it by right of inheritance."

"Your mother reproached me for not transmitting my looks to my daughters. She had little value for them in my case."

"Yes, it was a strange stroke of fate. I often think of the first impression we must make. Aunt Penelope perhaps makes a bridge between us. Some kind of stepping-stone is needed."

"So my appearance has its use, and my brother's has not," said her aunt. "It might hardly be the natural conclusion."

"It has indeed. And the conclusion might not be so unnatural. Ah, that nameless touch about you might be worth any handsomeness to some minds. Not to mine, as the father and daughter feeling stands in the way. But I can put myself in the other place. In my nature I am more drawn to a woman's quality than a man's."

"I have never been jealous of my sister," said Hereward. "I hope I may not be now. You must not find a way of coming between us."

"There could be no way. And I shall not seek one. I shall strive heart and soul to cement the bond. It is too great and precious a thing to be lightly assailed and weakened. You may trust me. In such a matter I am worthy of trust."

"In all matters," said Hereward, in a lower tone. "I will stay no longer to-day. I feel I should take no more. And indeed there is no more to take. I have gained the whole."

"You are wise, my dear?" said Alfred, when they were alone. "You had little time to think. And only under other eyes. And there is need for time and thought. The change is for your life."

"I am wise, Father. Indeed I am more. I am fortunate. I see it as a signal chance. I should not attract so many. I see myself as I am. And Hereward sees me as I am too. I shall not have to edit myself. There is no idealisation, and that is the line of safety. I am not in doubt."

36

"I think it would be better if there was some," said Emmeline. "I hope there will be for me."

"I daresay there will. I believe there might be now, if you had come to the age. I half-think I saw there would. If it was a few years later, I don't know how things would be."

"The years will pass," said Alfred. "You must see the matter from all its sides."

"Oh, I don't believe in roundabout views, Father. I look straight at a question, and feel that is enough. Aunt Penelope, let me have a word from you. What do you feel about having Hereward for a nephew?"

"For myself what goes without saying. As regards you I feel with your father."

"And a fair degree of feeling too. Not too much and not so little. A kind that may last and grow, when another might fade away. I am not a person for any strong romance. And I would not disturb the brother and sister relation, that I have viewed from a distance as something beyond myself. Now I am to be near to it, I shall go gently and keep a light touch. I shall not rush in where angels fear to tread."

"I would rather have something myself than be careful of it for other people," said Emmeline.

"I daresay you would. It is the difference between us. There is a strong vein of veneration in me. I am a person who tends to look up. I have looked up to one brother and sister, and now shall look up to another. They will feel they are safe with me, and it is a trust I value in them. And they will value my own trust. I also feel I am safe. I could hear their talk of me without a qualm."

This talk was proceeding, as the latter brother and sister went home.

"You are sure, Hereward? It was the work of a moment. It is to last to the end. It will change your daily life. You need to be sure, if you will ever need to."

"Yes, I am sure. I want to marry. I feel the urge, and it is time. Ada is goodhearted and will adapt her life to mine. She will accept our parents. She will be content with what I can give. There is much that I like about her. I need not say all that it is. She may hardly be a friend for you, but she will leave us our friendship. That is a condition I must make, and could not make with every woman. We are not asking nothing, Zillah. We can hardly ask more."

"Should you not have more? For yourself, if not for me? More for the years ahead? More foundation for all that is to come? Is it a better future for me than for you? I see it takes less from me than any other."

"Then it is the one for me. I will have nothing taken from you. No relation shall supersede our own. That is the one I will not do without. Only the woman to leave it to us can be my wife. I could not live with any other, would not ask her to live with me. My work is hard and never-ending. It will never end. I could not have another taskmistress. I serve only the one."

"How will you put it to our parents? Not in that way."

"No. You will put it for me as you please."

Zillah led the way to Sir Michael and his wife.

"I bring you some news. You are prepared for part. If you claim to have foreseen the rest, you must prove it."

Sir Michael spoke in a moment.

"My Zillah, I am prepared and not prepared. I knew it must come some day. And you have been going with your brother to the house. You act together, as you always do. And Merton is a good fellow and a good father. And as he has been a good husband, he will be so again. And if he was younger and not a widower, he would not be the man you choose. We cannot decide for other people, however near they may be. Joanna, come and wish our daughter all that is good. It is what she has always given."

"No, it is I who claim your feeling," said his son. "That is, if you have any over for me. It is Ada, not her father, who is to join our family. She is to be your

38

daughter as well as his. Zillah will remain with me. I could not lose her. I was startled by the picture that you drew."

"Then my congratulations, my son," said Sir Michael, holding out his hand. "We rejoice with you, if you rejoice. And of course you do. Your time has come for it. I remember when my own time came. And it is a good girl whom you have chosen, whom fate has thrown in your way. We must choose from the people we meet. We hunt in our own demesne. And the long friendship is a safeguard. It atones for not breaking up new ground. Ah, it is great news, the greatest we could have. It is true to say that words fail me, as I find they do."

"I am not quite sure they did," murmured Joanna. "Of course a mother's feelings are too deep for words. How sad it would be, if they were not!"

"You feel it is a humdrum marriage," said Hereward. "It may mean it is the one for me. It breaks no ground, as is said. I use my energy for other ends. It is safe and open and sound. It carries no doubt and no risk. It will not separate Zillah and me. We will leave you to see it as it is, as she and I and Ada see it."

"Michael, we have failed," said Joanna. "Failed our son in a crisis of his life. But it did not seem like a crisis, when it depended on dear Ada Merton. What do we feel about it? Well, you have said."

"I believe I did almost say it. I was taken by surprise. I wish I could re-live that moment. And that blunder I made about Zillah! What a thing to have said and un-said! I wish I could undo it. Not that any harm is done. She and Hereward are enough for each other. I only hope there will be something over for the wife. Well, she will not ask too much. She is a good, unexacting girl. I hope I did her justice. I hope I did not give a wrong impression."

"No, you gave the right one. Now all you can do is to erase it, knowing it can never be wholly effaced. I saw Hereward carrying it away with him."

"Tell me what you feel, Joanna."

"I could not tell anyone else. I am too ashamed of it. I am glad that Hereward can't like his wife any better than me. Because I don't see how he can. And glad that we may have grandchildren. All this selfish gladness, and then to have failed my son!"

"Well, Galleon," said Sir Michael. "You have not heard our news. Or have you heard? You look rather full of something."

"Some stray words did reach me, Sir Michael. I don't know if I gained the right impression."

"I daresay you did. So tell us what you feel."

"Well, it was a case of proximity, Sir Michael. That is how things must ensue, as I believe was said."

"So you listened to it all."

"I mentioned that some stray words reached me, Sir Michael. That happened to be one of them. I could have supplied it."

"We could not be more pleased with the marriage than we are."

"No, Sir Michael; it is a line of safety. There is the familiarity with everything. And so no uncertainty to come."

"Miss Ada is proud of Mr. Hereward's place in letters."

"Well, Sir Michael, it is even better, going so far."

"You would not go to the length yourself?"

"Well, Sir Michael, I have learned to go some way. I must suppress any personal bias. Sufferance is the badge of all my tribe."

CHAPTER IV

"Ring-a-ring-a-roses,
A pocket full of posies,
A-tish-a, a-tish-a,
All fall down."

Sɪʀ Mɪᴄʜᴀᴇʟ Eɢᴇʀᴛᴏɴ sank to the ground, and assisted
his wife to do the same, an example that was followed
by their three grandsons, with mirth in inverse proportion
to their age.

"Galleon fall down too," said the third, observing that
the butler was at leisure.

"No, Master Reuben, I have other things to do."

"No," said Reuben, as if seeing this was not the case.

"You can do them afterwards," said the second grandson.

"No, Master Merton, I have no time to waste."

"It seems as if you have," said the eldest.

"I know what I am doing, Master Salomon. You are
not old enough to understand."

"I am not, if you are really doing something."

"Galleon fall down too!" said Reuben, more insistently.

Sir Michael made a sign to Galleon, who complied
with openly simulated liveliness, resorting to the aid of
a chair, as if unconsciously.

"That is not falling," said Merton.

"Poor Galleon!" said Reuben, looking at him.

"It must be easy to be a butler," said Salomon. "It
would make other things seem hard."

"Nuts in May!" said Reuben, suddenly.

"Yes, that is an idea," said Sir Michael. "We must
choose our sides."

"Do we have to fall down?" said Joanna.

"No, my lady. Merely move forward and backward to the jingle," said Galleon, his choice of word shedding its light.

"Oh, what a good game! I wonder who invented it."

"I cannot say, my lady. Or to what purpose."

"There are not enough of us for sides," said Salomon.

"Yes, I think there are," said his grandfather. "You and I and Galleon on one, and Grandma and the little ones on the other."

"Salomon little too," said Ruben, at once.

"Not as little as you," said Merton.

"Yes, all the same," said Reuben, shrilly.

"Yes, all the same," said Salomon, in a pacific tone.

"Always all the same," said Reuben, sighing.

Salomon was a short, solid boy of seven, with a large, round head, a full, round face, wide, grey eyes and features resembling Sir Michael's. Merton, two years younger and nearly the same height, was a dark-eyed, comely boy with a likeness to Ada's father, whose name he bore. Reuben at three was puny for his age, with a pinched, plain face surprisingly like Emmeline's, considering the vagueness of feature of both.

"There are Father and Mother," said Merton.

"And Aunt Zillah, if Father is there," said Salomon.

"Well, that will swell our numbers," said Sir Michael. "And I hear your Aunt Emmeline too. It will give us a good game."

"Why are things called games?" said Salomon.

"I don't know," said Joanna. "It is not the right word."

"What would you call them?" said her husband.

"They are a kind of dance," said Merton.

"Something handed down," said his brother.

"Yes, they are old games," said Sir Michael. "Handed down to us from the past. I don't know their history."

"I am glad of that," said Joanna. "So no one else need know."

"Play again," said Reuben.

"Yes, in a minute," said his grandfather. "The others are on their way."

"All unknowing, my lady," said Galleon, with a smile for Joanna. "Or they might be disposed to divert it."

Hereward and his wife and sister entered, followed by the group from the other house. Alfred looked disturbed, Penelope grave, and Emmeline sober and aloof.

"Grandpa Merton play," said Reuben, laughing at the idea. "One, two grandpas play. Galleon grandpa too."

"No, Master Reuben. I have no little grandsons."

"He means you are old," said Salomon.

Galleon did not reply.

"No, Hereward, I can't put it off any longer," said Ada, in a tone that did not only address her husband. "I have tried to shut my eyes, but the time is past. I can't go on being blind and deaf and silent. I have eyes and ears, and now you will find I have words as well. You can feel you are finding it late. My father and aunt see the truth. Your father and mother see it. You and my sister know it in your hearts. Emmeline, my sister! To think what has come between us!"

"There need be nothing between you. No change has come to her or me. If there is a change, it is in you."

"It is true. No change has come. It was there from the first, the feeling between you. The change in me is that I see it. It is strange that I did not before. But I thought of her as a child."

"Of course the feeling was there. You were anxious that it should be. You put it in my heart. It was a thing we shared."

"No, something else is the truth. It helped your feeling for me. It went through everything. I see it now. I should have seen it then. You hardly hid it. It could not have been hidden from yourself."

"Why should I hide it? From myself or anyone else? I cared for you both. I do so now. What is there wrong about it?"

"We need not say," said Alfred. "But there is something that must be said. We know our world. We know its limits and its laws. We know they must be followed. We do not make our own."

"You need not think of me," said Emmeline. "I shall not be with you any longer. I am going away. I shall live at a distance from you all. Father and Aunt Penelope have arranged it. I see myself that I must go. I believe everyone would like me to stay. It is only that someone would like it too much."

"Oh, there it is!" said Ada, with a sigh. "As it has been, so it will always be. It is no good to talk of it. It must simply be accepted."

"I fear it must be," said her father, in the same grave tone. "And dealt with for the threat it carries, for the harm it does."

"Play game," said Reuben, as if matters had left their course.

"Yes, let us blow the cobwebs away," said Sir Michael.

"Cobwebs are light things," said Salomon, as though the word was not in place.

"And some things are not," said Ada. "Out of the mouth of babes! What would my sons say, if it was twenty years hence?"

"I know what to say now," said Salomon. "Father ought to love you, and not Aunt Emmeline."

"And I do love her," said Hereward. "And I love Aunt Emmeline too. And I love you and your brothers, and your aunt and your grandparents and others. So many people are dear to me, that I don't always judge between them."

"I think you will have to now. Mothers can't be quite the same. And you did judge in a way."

"Do you want to join in the game?" said Sir Michael, as if recognising evidence to the contrary.

"I would rather read. The game isn't a real one. It is only meant to hide something."

"Oh, we are all younger than he is," said Hereward. "Come, my three generations. We will leave our elder to himself."

"I want to hold Salomon's hand," said Reuben.

Salomon put down his book and went to his side.

" 'Here we come gathering nuts in May, nuts
    in May, nuts in May.
  Here we come gathering nuts in May, on a
    cold and frosty morning'."

Sir Michael rendered the words with abandon, and paused for Alfred to take him up on the other side.

"Whom will you have for your nuts in May?"
"We will have Ada for nuts in May—"
"Whom will you send to fetch her away—?"
"We will send Hereward to fetch her away, on
    a cold and frosty morning."

Hereward and Ada came into the centre to engage in the contest. Hereward was the victor and drew his wife to his own side. She fell against him and broke into tears, and her second son observed them and was disposed to add his own.

Her eldest gave them a glance.

"I knew it was not a game. It was the opposite of one."

"Well was it a success?" said Alfred. "I am not a judge."

"It was a success, Father," said Ada. "It has done its work. It has shown us things as they have to be, as we must see they are. We will leave it there."

"We will," said a quiet voice, as Penelope moved forward. "I think this scene is at an end. To continue it would avail us nothing. Emmeline will go home with her father, and will not come again. If the sisters say goodbye here and now, it will be said."

Emmeline suffered Ada's long embrace and Hereward's openly affectionate one, made little response to either, and followed her aunt.

"Play game," said Reuben, in a tone without much hope.

"No, a tale," said Merton. "Father always knows a new one."

"Not a new one," said Reuben, with a wail.

"I can tell you an old one," said Salomon. "Father can tell us one out of his head."

Hereward gathered his sons about him, taking Reuben on his knee, and threw himself into a narration that held them still and silent, and moved them to many human emotions, indeed to most of them.

"Again," said Merton, when it ended, keeping his eyes on his father's face.

"No, that should be enough, sir," said a voice from the door, where the nurse had stood with a dubious expression. "They will take some time to forget it."

"Is it only worthy of oblivion?"

"Well, that is really the best thing, sir," said Nurse in a candid tone. "It might prey on their minds."

"Again," said Merton, moving his feet rapidly.

"No, come and tell it to me," said Nurse. "I have only heard part of it."

"Yes," said Merton after a pause, a smile creeping over his face. "I will tell you it all."

Reuben waited on his father's knee until Nurse lifted him from it, indeed waited for her to do so. Merton followed them upstairs of his own will. It was where his treasure was, and where his heart was also. He was Nurse's favourite of the three brothers, and she was his favourite of all human beings.

Salomon sat down and opened his book, as a member of the remaining company.

"What a difficult book!" said his father. "Do you understand it?"

"I know it is an allegory. But I think of the people as real ones."

"Do you get any lessons from it? It is supposed to afford a good many."

"I am not old enough for them," said Salomon, meeting his father's eyes, as if this might not be true of everyone.

Hereward smiled to himself and went to the door.

"Well, it was a strange scene," said Sir Michael to his wife, waiting for it to close. "To take place before us all, as it did. I could scarcely believe my ears. I had a sense of eavesdropping somehow."

"I had not. Being obliged to hear something is so different from being tempted to hear it. It does not remind me of it."

"No, it has no zest about it. I don't mean the other would have any zest, of course. If we yielded to it, which we should not, of course. Well, it was an unusual scene."

"Oh, I daresay I have cut a sorry figure," said Ada, with another sigh. "But I felt the time had come, and that it was then or never. In marrying an ordinary woman Hereward has involved himself with an ordinary woman's feelings. But I have talked enough about my ordinariness. You are well aware of it. You know Hereward has not married a martyr. And you see that I have not either."

"You have not married an ordinary man," said Zillah. "You must meet much that is not ordinary. He can only be a rule to himself."

"But only in his own sense. A gifted person owes as much to other people as an average one. Surely not any less."

"You can hardly feel that Hereward has not fulfilled his human debt."

"His debt to his wife is part of it. He has a duty to her as well as to the public. Or I am one of the public, if you like."

"No, do not be one," said Joanna. "I am sure I am not, though I don't dare to give the reasons."

"Well, I dare for you, Mamma," said Ada. "I dare to give many. And one of them is the way you have behaved to-day. Taking no sides, understanding everyone, condemning no one. Just there to help by being the whole of yourself. What better reason is there?"

47

Before an answer was necessary, Hereward returned to the room. He wore an absent air and was humming to himself.

"Still at the book?" he said to his son. "Don't you get rather tired of it?"

"I don't read it all the time. I don't like the second part."

"You have not been listening to grown-up talk?" said Ada, with a note of reproof.

"It was the only kind there was. Of course I have heard it."

"Are you any the wiser?" said Hereward.

"Yes, I think I am a little."

"Tell us what you have learned from it."

"It would be no good to tell you. You must know it yourself."

"Why, this is a son after your heart, Hereward," said Sir Michael. "Do you begin to see yourself in him?"

"He likes Reuben best," said Salomon.

"That is a different kind of feeling," said his father.

"I think there is only one kind."

"I am a lover of very young children. You would hardly understand."

"I think I am too," said Salomon, smiling at his own words. "I like Reuben myself."

"My feeling for all of you grows with every day."

"I thought it had got less for me."

"That is because you don't understand it."

"It might be because I do. And I think it is. There isn't much in a feeling to understand. It is just something that is there."

"You must not argue with Father," said Ada. "He must be wiser than you are."

"I can't help not thinking what he does. It is a thing no one can help. It is only he and Aunt Zillah who always think the same."

"Ah, that is what they do," said Sir Michael. "And

a great thing for both of them it is. Neither will ever stand alone. They can always be left to each other. Indeed they might be now. They deserve an hour to themselves. We all acknowledge their right to it."

"Come then, my little son," said Ada. "We will go upstairs and give our minds to the young children. Father is leaving them to us."

"And trusting them to their mother with an easy heart," said Sir Michael, in a full tone, as he left the room. "He is making no mistake there."

"Well, it was a thunderbolt, Zillah," said Hereward. "I was taken by surprise. It all seemed to fall from nowhere."

"I have wondered if it would come. And it has come and gone, and will not come again. But what will it mean? What will you do without Emmeline?"

"Think of her, and write to her, and know why I have no answer. They can't take everything from me. And they can't take you. They do not dare to think of it. Ada would not wish to have me without my sister."

"Nor you to have her without hers. And that has to end. But she can be accepted in herself. She does not give us nothing."

"To me it is more than that. I have a value for all that she gives. I have not lost my feeling for her. I will not lose it. I guard it more closely than my feeling for you. It is not so safe. And much depends on it."

"I will help you to keep it. You need not fear. In a sense it is at the root of our life. It is the basis of the future and the safeguard of it."

"Zillah, we are brother and sister. If we were not, what could we be?"

"Nothing that was nearer. It stands first among the relations. There is nothing before it, nothing to follow it. It reaches from the beginning to the end."

"Well, I may or may not be welcome," said Ada's voice. "But I must assert myself once more. There are things I can and do accept. But banishment from my husband in my own home is not one of them."

"My father's words mean nothing," said Hereward. "We have ceased to listen to them, almost to hear them. You must learn to do the same."

"I know they meant nothing to him. Why, he and I are fast friends. His presence is often a help to me. To-day it enabled me to break my silence. To do what was beyond myself. And it was time it was broken. There had ceased to be a case for it."

"Whether or no that is true," said Zillah, "I think there is a case for it now."

"Oh, well, I am willing. I don't want to press things home. There is too much of the fairness of the ordinary person in me for that. Something had to be ended, and it is at an end. I shall not return to it. But I don't feel with you about your father. I like to hear his voice, sounding cheerfully about, expressing goodwill to everyone. I hear it now; and if it cannot be music in my ears, it is something that is no less welcome."

The voice was coming across the hall, gaining volume as it drew near.

" 'Here we come gathering nuts in May, nuts in May, nuts in May. Here we come gathering nuts in May on a cold and frosty morning.

" 'A touch of frost in the nuts in May, nuts in May, nuts in May. A touch of frost in the nuts in May, on a cold and frosty morning.

" 'Ah, we managed to smooth it away, smooth it away, smooth it away. Ah, we managed to smooth it away, on a cold and frosty morning'.

"Oh, there you all are! How that jingle sounds in one's head! The tune that is, of course. The words have no meaning."

"Can that ever be said of words?" said Zillah to her brother.

CHAPTER V

"WELL, THE BOOK is ended," said Hereward. "What there can be in a word! I am in a strange solitude. I seem to move in a void. I am without any foothold, any stake in life. I have suffered it before, and it is never different. I have had and done what I wanted. But I pay the price."

"Come, what of your home and your family?" said Sir Michael. "What is this talk of a void? You have the stake in life of other men."

"I have lost my own. The people have left me, who have lived with me and made my world. More deeply than mere flesh and blood."

"You mean you have finished with them? And mere flesh and blood! What are you or any of us? What of your mother and me? What of your characters themselves? They are supposed to be like real people. I thought that was the point of them. It is what is often said. Indeed I have thought—" Sir Michael broke off and glanced about him, a smile trembling on his lips.

"I don't use my family as characters, if that is what you mean. They would serve no purpose for me."

"Well, not as characters, not in your sense I daresay. But things here and there—little touches—I have thought —" Sir Michael leaned back and smiled again to himself.

"*Mere* flesh and blood!" said Salomon to his father. "And Grandpa before your eyes!"

"Well, I am the man I am," said Sir Michael, modestly. "I have my thoughts and perceptions like anyone else. Or like myself I suppose. It may come from being flesh and blood. That is, of one's own kind."

"I daresay a good deal comes from that," said Merton.

"Well, I return to your world," said Hereward. "I have lost my own. I am happy in having had it. But I would not urge another man to follow in my steps. I do not wish it for my sons. It is a hard path to tread."

"It seems that it has its allure," said Salomon. "I don't feel it myself. Or perhaps feel that of any other."

"Well, you are in a place apart. You will not have to earn your bread. Your brothers must think of the future. I shall not live and write for ever."

"To think that I must tread a path!" said Reuben.

"And earn bread," said Merton. "What a hard and frugal course! It is a malicious phrase."

"Have you thought of a way of gaining it?" said Hereward. "What of your work in the years ahead?"

"Well, I know the main line, Father. I can put it in a few words. I want to be a writer. But not of your range and kind. I should not appeal to the many, and shall be content to write for the few. But by them, in this country and beyond it, I hope to be known in the end. And not only known; read."

There was a silence.

"It ought hardly to have been in a few words," said Salomon.

"But it is in those that good writers suggest so much," said Joanna.

Hereward was silent, and his father gave him a glance.

"Why should I not speak the truth?" said Merton, looking at them. "It was a simple thing that I said."

"Simple in a sense you did not mean," said Hereward, in an even tone.

"You have had a writer's life yourself. You should not feel it a strange one for your son."

"You spoke of a different one from mine."

"You feel I should follow in your steps? But we cannot choose our paths. They are chosen for us by something in ourselves. As yours was for you, and mine is for me. There can be no family custom there."

52

"I find no fault with your path. I am glad you have chosen one. It is what I hoped for you. But what do you mean by the few?"

"You will know, if you think. I have heard you use the phrase. A small part of your books is read by them. It is they I should write for, and hope to reach; and feel I should in the end."

" 'In this country and beyond it'," said his father, as if to himself.

"Oh, you think it is too ambitious. To choose the better part, if that is what it is; and I admit I think it is. But it might be thought narrower than yours, and by some it would be. Our abilities are different, and must lead to a different end. It is not unreasonable to think it. But it is rather in the air at my age."

"It is not only in the air. It is in your thought. And your age perplexes me. Sixteen is hardly childhood."

"Yes, in this matter, Hereward," said Zillah. "It is what it is."

"I wonder what fourteen is," said Reuben. "I will not talk of it, in case someone tells me."

"Anything worth knowing is known by my age," said Merton. "Sixteen may be the high mark of youth. After that there can be retrogression as well as progress."

"Father is deprived of words," said Salomon.

Hereward was silent, as this was the case.

"Seventy-nine is not what it is," said Joanna. "Or it would be old age."

"Neither is it," said Sir Michael. "I feel as young as I ever did."

"I do not," said Reuben. "I must begin to realise my age. I have to know all that is worth knowing in two years."

"Childhood does take us quickly onward," said Zillah.

"So it does," said Hereward, lightly. "We see where it has taken Merton. Beyond his father."

"That is the idea that troubles you, Father? But there is nothing so unusual about it."

"Nothing. It is its commonness that strikes me. I have seen the death of hope."

"You have also seen its fulfilment. And met it yourself in a sense. Of course I don't know what your original ambitions were."

"We shall not say that of yours. And, as you have said, I am troubled by them. Both as a writer and a father. What are your hopes for the future, Reuben?"

"I have none, Father, only fears. And one of them is that I may be an usher. It is one that does take the place of hopes."

"Why do we say 'usher' and not 'schoolmaster'?" said Sir Michael. "It has a disparaging sound."

"That is the reason," said his grandson. "We should hardly admit a note of respect."

"Why not?" said Hereward. "Education has its purpose and serves it. I wish I had had more."

"You would not have it," said his father. "You said it would crush your creative gifts."

"You can't be an usher without it," said Salomon. "So I suppose ushers' gifts are always crushed. Before we have the advantage of them."

"I wonder we risk education," said Reuben, "when you think where it might lead. You will all remember that my gifts have been crushed."

"That does not happen so easily," said Merton. "People are without them, because they have never had them. If they had, they would not be ushers. And the lack of talent in many writers is a part of themselves. Of course I am not talking about Father."

"Well, I suppose you are not," said Sir Michael. "Why should you be?"

"I wonder he was not," said Hereward, smiling. "But I have a word to say of him. They are all to go to Oxford, when they reach the age. It is their mother's wish, and therefore mine."

"Yes, my word was the determining factor," said Ada.

54

"I brought in the ordinary strain. That is my accepted part. My sons cannot follow in their father's steps. They must see him as widely removed from them, as my sister and I saw mine. They must have the usual training of average men. Why should they be above them? We should not hope, or perhaps even wish for it."

"There are cases of a literary father and son," said Merton. "And either of them may be the better. But it is idle to plan the future. It must take care of itself."

"I did not find it did," said Hereward. "The effort fell to me. I found it a long, hard service. And you may do the same. I even hope you will. It might be better for you in the end."

"Why are early struggles so much recommended? They may not lead to success, because they end in it."

"Well, may you do all you hope, my boy. No one would be prouder than your father."

"No one is prouder of you, than I am in my way, Father. Of course it must be in my way. Our opinions and aims are different. They would hardly be the same."

"I thought aims were always the same," said Joanna. "And I believe they are."

"They are more so than is thought," said Zillah. "They tend to meet, as time goes by. They are adapted to achievements, and those do come nearer to each other."

"Have you found that true, Father?" said Merton.

"I think there is truth in it. But I have never been concerned with aims. We give out what is in us."

"Is not that saying the same thing?"

"I daresay it is," said Joanna. "It so often is, when people say different things."

"Let us leave our aims," said Salomon. "I like to forget them, as I have none. Mother, you spoke of your sister. Why has she passed from our lives? I remember so well when she was in them."

"She lives at a distance," said Hereward. "And her marriage has widened it, as marriages will."

"My Emmeline!" said Ada. "I hardly feel I have lost her. Reuben gives her back to me. And more with every day."

"There is a great likeness," said Zillah. "And it seems to grow with him. I suppose a real likeness would."

"It is not only in his looks and ways. There is something that defies words. It is the touch I have missed myself. It is impossible to define it. I don't know if it will lead anywhere."

"That would need something with more depth and force," said Merton.

"I don't think Merton has a touch," said Reuben.

"It is an elusive thing," said Ada. "We can't give it a place."

"We have given it one," said Reuben. "It is in Aunt Emmeline and me."

"Aunt Emmeline! How natural it sounds! How I wish we had heard it oftener!"

"Why have we not?" said Merton. "Why do we never see her? There must be a private reason. I suppose some family trouble."

"There is or there was," said his mother. "So that is enough."

"But it is not," said Salomon. "Not nearly enough, as you know."

"We can add to it," said Merton. "I expect it had to do with money."

"You are wrong," said Hereward. "Money is not the whole of life."

"It is often the whole of quarrels, Father."

"It was no part of this one."

"I am surprised that there was trouble, Father," said Salomon. "I remember you and my aunt together."

"There was no trouble between her and me."

"Perhaps it was the opposite," said Merton. "Ah, that is nearer the truth."

"So it is out," said Ada. "Well, it had to come. Questions are asked in the end, and carry their answers. Yes, your father and my sister were becoming too much to each other. And it led to a breach that has remained. Not an estrangement, not a silence. But a parting of the ways."

"How I long to ask a question!" said Reuben.

"Well, what is it?" said his father.

"What do you feel for Aunt Emmeline now?"

"I keep the memory. I cared both for her and your mother. I cared for them both for each other's sake and their own. We fell in with your mother's wish and parted. She married later. That is the whole."

"My wish!" said Ada. "No, it is not quite the whole. Both my father and Aunt Penelope advised the parting. But my sister! How I wish it had been different! I hope and feel so does she. But nothing can be undone."

"It seems that this might be ended," said Salomon. "Do you need to remember the past?"

"Now that is enough," said Sir Michael. "Your parents have told you all they can. You should know better than to ask more."

"Well, we will be content. It is a relief to know. I have wondered and feared to ask."

"So have I," said Merton. "It has been on the tip of my tongue."

"That does keep people silent," said Joanna. "It hardly seems that it would."

"Well, the truth has escaped, Grandma. I admire Mother's simple courage. It is a thing I am without."

"And you admire yourself for being without it," said Ada. "It may not be a high quality. But it is not such a common one."

"I think it is," said Reuben. "I am always meeting it."

"I have to show it now," said Hereward. "I am reluctant to cloud our reunion. That is how it seems to me when I leave a book. But there is a word that must be said. Your reports are here and cannot be quite passed over."

"Well, now they have not been," said Reuben. "We have met the courage."

57

"Yours was no worse than mediocre."

"That is right for me, as I am to educate others. If it was better, I should not educate them. And if it was worse, I could not."

"There is never any fault to be found with yours, Salomon."

"None by you, Father. I am steady and of sound intelligence. But they are things that Merton would be ashamed to be."

"He has his own cause to be ashamed. His is hardly a report at all. It seems there was little to make one. He is said to assume he is a man before his time. He may not have to educate others. But he can hardly do without education himself."

"So you think I could be improved, Father?"

"It appears to be what is thought."

"Not by prolonging boyhood. Education so-called does only what it can."

"And does idleness so-called do so much?" said Sir Michael. "And does ingratitude so-called do any more? Things have to be known by their names. Why should your father immure himself and moil, for you to be a man before your time? 'So-called' is the right word there. Why, I am ashamed of being your grandparent."

"I am not," said Joanna. "I don't see how I can help it."

"Well, I have done what I can," said her husband, leaning back. "No one can do any more."

"That is good to hear," said Merton. "I was fearing you might go to almost any length."

"Any length! Well, I went a certain way. I felt it was my part. It is my duty to second your father. I see it as the least I can do. The brunt of things falls on him. I take any chance to support him."

"Well, I give you one by speaking the truth. I am not afraid of it. I can't be a slave to what is called my work. I know where my real talent lies, and what I owe to it."

"What is called your work! Is everything to be so-called? What do you do with your so-called leisure, may I ask? Perhaps it is the word there."

"It is. I give it to the writing that is to be my life, and to last it. And not more for my own sake than for other people's."

"Oh, well, for other people's. Well, if that is what it is. Well, it is a thing I am used to. I am no stranger to it. This working for the world outside, and forgetting the one you live in. Like father, like son, I suppose. Well, we must not find fault with it."

"I fear I must," said Hereward. "Though I may not seem the person to do it. I am troubled for Merton's future. The likeness between us is not so great. It should have a better basis than these early efforts and hopes."

"What basis did you have for your own, Father?"

"That of a stronger brain and greater creative force," said Hereward, in an almost ruthless tone. "I will say the truth, as you do. It is time it was said. We are right not to be afraid of it."

"But just afraid enough," murmured Salomon.

"I am terrified," murmured Reuben.

"I am untouched," said their brother. "If it is the truth to you, you are right to say it, Father. It is the honest thing. Indeed I admire your courage."

"I admire Merton's," said Salomon.

"But I have no fear. There are different kinds of brain. The one that is known as powerful, may not be the best."

"You would not like to have written my books?" said Hereward, meeting his eyes.

"Well, to be as honest as you are, Father. I should not."

"We are told not to be afraid of the truth," said Joanna. "But no one is."

"No one who speaks it," said Reuben. "Everyone else."

"The people who speak it can be the most afraid," said Hereward. "But at times it must be said."

"There is nothing in Merton's feeling," said Zillah.

"No writer goes the whole length with any other. Each

of them shivers at the lapses of the rest, and is blind to his own. And the youngest shiver the most. And the greatest writers have them."

"And I daresay the smaller ones too," said Sir Michael. "And a boy who would not like to have written a mature man's books, is a queer example of one to my mind. Why, I should like to have written them myself. I should be proud to have written a word. And he can think what he likes of it."

"I think it is quite reasonable, Grandpa."

"The less we can do a thing ourselves, the more we should appreciate it in other people. To fail is to grudge someone else the better place. We should be ashamed of it."

"Grandpa need not be ashamed," said Reuben. "He tells us about it."

"Well, I need not either," said Merton. "I simply want to write for a body of readers neglected because it is small. It is not an unworthy ambition."

"I am sure it is not," said Joanna. "An ambition would not be. Nothing can be said against ambitions. They are worthier than anything I know."

"Not unworthy on its narrow scale," said Sir Michael. "But there is something more generous about serving the larger body. It commands more sympathy."

"It is true that it does," said Merton.

"I can't think a son of mine would go far along either road," said Ada. "There is too much of myself in them. My father's gifts are of another kind, but they too have passed them over."

"It is a habit of gifts," said Salomon.

"But broken in Merton's case," said Reuben.

"Not by the second kind," said their brother. "I lay no claim to that. The two kinds of gifts are wide apart, and the gulf is seldom crossed."

"Well, it need not concern us," said his mother. "For us the gulf may be all there is."

"Well, that may be true," said Sir Michael, laughing.

"Gifts must be rare, of course. But to have a father and a grandfather endowed like theirs is a unique position. Ah, they have a fine heritage. Something ought to come of it."

"Merton has come," murmured Reuben.

"Still we can't choose the kind of people we are to be."

"Some of us feel we can," said Hereward.

"If you are thinking of me, you are wrong," said Merton. "I know what I am, as everyone must. How can we escape the knowledge?"

"Mr. and Miss Merton," said Galleon at the door.

"Why, Father, you were in my mind," said Ada. "I was thinking of your having only daughters. We are facing the future for our sons. And daughters are allowed to disregard it."

"I would have faced it for and with any sons of mine."

"Father, you have had a disappointment! How wonderfully you have hidden it! How grateful we ought to be!"

"Father and Mother have had one," said Reuben. "And I suppose it could hardly be hidden. It was me."

"Yes, I did want a daughter," said Ada. "But I would not change my sons. Or change anything about them."

"Father should emulate a mother's feelings," said Merton. "They are much respected."

"What about you, Aunt Penelope?" said Ada. "Would you have liked to have great-nieces?"

"I am content with what has come to me. I have taken no steps myself."

"And how grateful for it we should be! Ah, our unmarried women! Where should we be without them? What a place they fill!"

"It is not always so highly considered."

"Oh, but it is. By people who take the broader view. And in this matter they are many. What would Father say about it?"

"The place I fill for him was left empty. That is how I came to be in it."

61

"Honest and clear as always! How we should miss the light you shed! There will be a void one day."

"You don't mean that she will die?" said Joanna. "You know she will not. You must know no one will, who is here."

"I mean that she will live on in our memories and our lives, as long as we breathe ourselves. That is what I mean."

"It is what you suggested," said Hereward.

"Oh, you are a sardonic, carping creature to-day. You are not fair on anyone. If the boys want to escape to their own sanctum, you must not blame them. They may have had enough of you."

"I should not blame them. I daresay they have had too much. They can go and forget us. And we will go our several ways."

"Well, Galleon," said Sir Michael. "You have heard the talk. What do you say to a second writer in the family?"

"Well, 'like father, like son', as was said, Sir Michael. Or that at the moment. It is a stage that may pass."

"And you feel it better that it should?"

"Well, one irregularity in the family, Sir Michael. It is no great thing."

"You still see writing in that way?"

"Well, hardly Mr. Alfred Merton's, Sir Michael. Involving what it does. This of ours is of a lighter nature," said Galleon, trying to take a step forward.

"But that is not against it."

"On the contrary, Sir Michael. It has its own purpose."

"Well, you know, Galleon," said Sir Michael, lowering his tone and glancing round the empty room, "I half-feel it myself. There might be something more solid, and without the personal touch. But I am wrong you know. Utterly off the truth. I understand that now. And there is no prouder father."

"And there is no point in a prouder butler, Sir Michael," said Galleon, smiling. "There would be no place for pride."

"And we welcome the help with expenses. They grow with every year."

"I have heard of a lady who made a fortune by the type of writing, Sir Michael," said Galleon, with another effort to adapt himself.

"Well, I hope my grandson will make one. And in the same way. Though there seems somehow to be a doubt of it."

The grandsons had gone to the room that was known as their study, on the assumption that it earned the name. They took their accustomed seats and leaned back in silence.

"Strength will return," said Salomon at last. "We have found it does. What if a time came, when it did not?"

"For me it has come," said Merton. "Virtue has gone out of me."

"It has," said Reuben. "We saw and heard it going out. I suppose you will never smile again. I hardly feel that I shall."

"Father will not, if I follow in his sacred steps. No one else is to tread in them."

"Is anyone else able to?" said Salomon. "It is on that score that he is troubled."

"He may feel some doubt of his work, and not welcome a competitor."

"Whom does he see in that light? His doubt takes another direction."

"He must be conscious of his failings. He may feel that I may avoid them."

"He is conscious of other things that you may avoid."

"I would rather write nothing than write as he does."

"Well, that should offer no problem."

"I have already written, you know."

"Nothing we may see. We could all say that."

"Well, the future will show."

"I can't bear the future," said Reuben. "Why must we always harp on it?"

"There is a past as well," said Merton. "We have

had new light on Father's. No wonder you are his favourite, with your likeness to Aunt Emmeline. We feel how little we have known him. And feel there may be more to know. We can see that the trouble lives in Mother's memory."

"That would not matter," said Salomon. "But it lives in Father's."

"He ought to have a strange, mixed feeling for me," said Reuben. "Perhaps he has."

"His feeling is mixed for all of us," said Merton. "It is not pure fatherly affection, as we have seen."

"No, it is also anxiety and fear for your future," said Hereward's voice. "You are taking hasty steps on the path of life. I watch them with misgiving."

"You know what it is to have taken them," said Merton.

"And so do not want you to know it. You will be wise to move with care. The forces about us are many. We have need of a sure foothold."

"I wish Father would not talk as he writes," murmured Merton, looking down.

"We write from within," said Hereward, keeping his eyes on his son. "We write as we feel and live. It is the way to be honest and ourselves. It is as ourselves that all is done."

"I have no doubt that I shall write as myself, Father."

"My boy, I wish you would. I hope you will. But you may be afraid of the natural springs and deeps. If you are, you fear yourself."

"We must know ourselves to write as them," said Salomon. "And that might arouse fear."

"It means we must have courage," said Hereward, as he closed the door.

"We often need it," said Merton. "I feel I have shown it to-day."

"We feel with you," said Salomon. "We wondered how much you would show. We did not show it. But we had to have it."

CHAPTER VI

"WELL, I HAVE a word to say," said Merton at the table, using a conscious tone and throwing up his brows. "It may cause some surprise."

"It can only cause me pleasure," said his mother. "I wondered if we should ever hear a word from you again."

"A voice from the silence," said Reuben. "With a strangely familiar sound."

"I have had to give some thought to my own life. It is a thing that no one will do for me. And I am about to tell you the result. You can hardly guess it."

"You have had a book accepted," said Reuben. "No, we should hardly have guessed it. I do feel some surprise."

"I have not offered one. And when I spoke of my own life, I meant something that went deeply into it."

"Your books should do that," said Hereward. "If they are to find a place in other lives."

"You are going to be married?" said Ada. "No, no, my boy, you are too young."

"Women and their wits!" said Merton. "How these things are true! But you are only partly right. I am twenty-four."

"That may confirm what your mother said," said Hereward. "And how will you support a wife?"

"When you have not had a book accepted," said Reuben.

"It is not a joke," said Merton. "I don't know why you think it is."

"Your becoming a family man! What else can it be?"

"And the support of a family!" said Salomon. "There is no reason for thinking it a joke."

There was a pause.

"I am going to hang up my hat in my wife's hall," said Merton.

There was another pause.

"I always think that sounds so comfortable," said Joanna. "And then you will go in to her fire."

"Yes, that is what I should do," said Reuben.

"Ah, ha! So should I," said Sir Michael. "And that is not all it would be. Let us hear about everything."

"Yes, tell us the whole," said Herward. "It concerns us as much as it does you. We are deeply involved, my boy."

"My son, may it all go well with you," said Ada.

"It sounds as if it is doing so," said Salomon.

"It is going well," said Merton, in an even tone. "I am happier than I thought I could be. And I welcome the material ease. It is a great thing, as you all agree. She is an orphan, without near relations, and has inherited the family money. I feel no scruple in sharing it. I am taking deeper things. And we must be able to accept."

"We most of us are," said Salomon. "And we must be, as you say. I have always been equal to it."

"You earn what you take, by filling my place," said Hereward. "It enables other people to accept."

"She will take something herself," said Reuben. "Merton will provide the relations. I hope she will find me a brother."

"I shall have a daughter," said Ada. "It will be a long wish fulfilled. How it makes us talk of ourselves! But Merton knows our hearts."

"I shall go on with my writing," said her son. "I hope I shall go further with it. It will be a help to feel there is no haste. It should mean work of a deeper quality."

"Urgency is said to be a stimulant," said Salomon. "It seems it is not a dependable one."

"Writing is not breaking stones," said his brother.

"That sounds as if it must be true," said Joanna.

"It is only partly so," said Hereward. "Everything is breaking stones, up to a point."

"When are we to meet her?" said Ada. "What a moment it will be!"

"I have asked her to dinner to-morrow," said Merton. "And we will ask Grandpa Merton and Aunt Penelope. And kill all the birds with one stone."

"There are a good many birds," said Joanna. "I feel rather ashamed of being one."

"Will you be living near to us?" said Zillah. "The questions must follow each other."

"Not far away. In the house in the bend of the hills. The small one in the curving road."

"I don't call it small. How your ideas are enlarging! And at what a pace!"

"My son, it is a great step," said Hereward. "You will let us take it with you? There is indeed a place for her."

"Would you be annoyed if I asked her name?" said Salomon. "I don't mean it as a joke. Everyone has one."

"Yes, even I have," said Reuben. "But I feel it is rather a joke."

"You will know it to-morrow. And part of it will cease to be hers."

"And may we ask her age? She has lived for some years, as we all have."

"I hardly know it. That is, I am not quite sure. It is a little more than mine, and so will balance the lack in it."

"You can now be any age you please," said Zillah. "It is true that everything has to be paid for."

"Well, Merton has outdistanced you, Salomon," said Sir Michael. "The one of you who seemed at a standstill. That is, there hasn't been much about him of late."

"It is no great feat, as I am always at a standstill."

"I am not," said Reuben. "I take my brave, little steps forward."

"I feel I have outdistanced everyone," said Merton. "I am uplifted to a height I had not known."

67

"Well, make the most of it," said Sir Michael. "It will not last. Well, we hope it will. I mean, may it last, of course."

"How quickly you have found a house!" said Ada. "Have you been looking for one?"

"No, it is her own. She is living in it. I shall join her there. When I said I should hang up my hat in my wife's hall, I meant it."

"Well, your path is smooth," said Sir Michael. "It might have been a rough one, as your parents feared."

"It might. And I should still have taken it. I am not blind to my good fortune."

"Merton is softened, like his path," said Reuben.

"As he would be," said Zillah. "We must be influenced by the ways we take."

"Well, the hour of the meeting will come," said Sir Michael. "It is an exciting thought. We have had no change in the family since Reuben was born. And that wasn't much, as he was a third son."

"Fate was against me from the first," said his grandson. "I have trodden a hard way. It is really quite dignified."

The hour came, and with it Alfred and Penelope to meet the newcomer. She was a tall, dark, quiet young woman, clearly more mature than Merton, with straight, rounded features, large, dark eyes, and a way of looking fully into people's faces, as if in appreciation and interest. Merton was too sure of her appeal to show more than his usual consciousness.

"Well, here is the patriarch, my grandfather; his consort, my grandmother; his son, my father; his daughter-in-law, my mother; his daughter, my aunt. Oh, and his grandsons, my brothers."

"I did not know I was a consort," said Joanna. "Then I think Ada must be one."

"I have avoided the stigma," said Penelope. "And have had no credit for it."

"My maternal great-aunt, Miss Merton; my maternal grandfather, also of the name."

"Are we not to hear another name?" said Ada. "The one we are waiting to hear."

"It is *Hetty*," said its owner, in quiet, even tones. "The only one to all of you. The other I am going to share with you. I must learn that it is mine."

"There will be more for you to share," said Sir Michael. "We will give you all we can."

"It cannot be much," said Hetty, smiling. "What you have can only be your own."

"I would give all I could," said Joanna. "But I can't think of anything."

Hetty laughed, with her eyes on Joanna's face.

"You make such a difference to so many people. You are making it to me."

"It is a thing that will be true of you," said Salomon. "I hope Merton will let me say it."

"I knew he would not let me," said Reuben. "So I had to waste it. It did come into my mind."

"Merton's parents await judgement," said Hereward, standing by his wife. "We need not speak of the one we have made."

"Neither need I," said Hetty. "I envy Merton the background to his life. It must mean so much to have one."

"Well, now it will be yours," said Sir Michael. "With everything else that is his."

"I feel less poor already. I see how poor I have been."

"My brothers' names can come later," said Merton. "When we have had some meat and drink."

Sir Michael led Hetty to the head of the dinner table. Merton sat by her, and the others fell at random into place. Alfred and Hereward were opposite to Hetty, and found her resting her eyes on them.

"What a pair to have before me! I am not used to people on the heights."

"Merton does not see me in that way," said Hereward. "He thinks lightly of his father's place."

"It may be too far removed from him. It is yours and belongs to yourself. He must see it from a distance, and judge it as he can."

"You do not put him above us all in everything?"

"I put him in the place he is right to fill. The place that is his own."

"What do you say to it, Merton?" said Salomon.

"Oh, Hetty is not versed in such things as yet. She is content to be simply herself. She never pretends to be anything she is not."

"You are brought to this! I have no conception of your state."

"No, I can see you have none."

"You are my first grand-daughter," said Alfred. "And I am your second grandfather. I must seem to you a superfluous figure."

"How can I say what you are? What do I know of you and your work? What can I know?"

"What of me and my work?" said Hereward, in a lower tone, as his son looked aside. "Have you not your knowledge there?"

"Yes, I have," said Hetty, meeting his eyes. "But it is still only mine. Merton's time for it has not come. We don't know the whole of each other yet."

"Would you dare to tell him the truth?"

"I have dared to tell him part. And he recognised my courage and disputed my judgement. But he will grow towards it. I am older than he is, you know."

"Surely not much," said Alfred.

"Five years. A good deal for a woman over a man. I should be content to go further than he does. I have gone further."

"And you are content?" said Hereward, smiling. "And so am I."

"Come, come, you elderly men," said Sir Michael.

"Is Merton to have a share of his future wife? Or are you taking his place?"

"They have their own place, as he has," said Hetty. "And I am learning mine."

"She has a liking for men two or three times her age," said Merton. "It is a tribute to me that she accepted a younger one."

"They may have a liking for her," said Sir Michael. "They can see age in their own way."

"I would ask no one's opinion of her. I have my own."

"My daughter!" said Ada. "It would be safe to ask mine."

"I might say the same," said Hetty, meeting her eyes. "Indeed I have said it. To myself, when I first came in."

"I must appear another superflous figure," said Penelope.

"Well, luxuries may seem superfluous things. But they can be among the best."

"What will you say of me?" said Zillah. "I am more of a problem. Even you may be at a loss."

"I will say nothing. What can I say? To you, to whom we owe everything, even the great man himself."

"What is that?" said Hereward, as they left the room, seeming just to catch the words. "Yes, we may talk to each other. We are not to separate to-night. We are all to have our share of you. And I will have mine. Tell me what the talk was about."

"Why should I tell you what you know?"

"Well, I will understand you. And it was not Merton's voice I heard."

"No, it was mine. I know his would be his own. I know his work is different from yours. I wish it was not. And he does not see yours as I do. I wish he did. I wish he could see it as it is."

"Well, with you I wish he could. As much as would be of use to him. It need be no more. I would not be of use to me. And I do not serve myself."

71

"He may in the end. It seems he must."

"I think he will not. And I do not ask it. I would ask nothing to which I had no right. We have none to be looked up to."

"Some of us have earned it. We know you are among them."

"Not in my own family. I have earned it in many others. I am what is called a household word. It is what I wanted and have had. My son has other hopes. He has told you what they are." Hereward smiled and then let his voice get fuller. "My wish is to reach the multitude, to go deeper into many hearts. I think it comes from a deeper one. It meets a greater need."

"The difference in Merton may be in himself. His aims must come from his powers, as everyone's must. They may be nearer to yours as they grow. And that will show him their distance."

"Ah, I should have had a daughter. I have always known it."

"You will have one now. And you will have others through your other sons."

"I only want one. It is what I need. It is the classic relation, rooted in the past. My wife has done much for me. But now all she can do. And my sons go their distance, and can go no further."

"It must be true of all of them. It would have to be."

"Yes, I should remember. You will help me not to forget. I know what they have to give. They do not fail to give it. I myself can say no more."

"You always have your sister?"

"We have gone through life together. She goes with me still. She will always go with me. I have no doubt of her. And my wife has not grudged us to each other. I have had all I could from both."

"And now you will have something from me. On my own small scale."

"It will be what I want, what I have not had. You

72

will come to me often, come when I am thought to be alone. It is what a daughter would do."

"What are you saying, Hereward?" said Ada. "You will bewilder Hetty and ask too much of her. You have no right to ask anything yet. You are going too fast and too far. Merton is turning his eyes on you."

"I am taking what he gives me. We do not reject a gift."

"I have become so many things," said Hetty. "And I am still only myself."

"I can't say he has given me a sister," said Reuben. "He might turn his eyes on me."

"Do you feel you can say it?" said Hetty, smiling at Salomon, whose voice had been more seldom heard.

"Well, it is all a matter of Merton's eyes."

"He is giving me a grand-daughter," said Joanna. "But I am not sure that he thought of it. I believe he just meant to give himself a wife."

"So you need not show your gratitude," said Salomon. "And it might be a false step."

"I shall not show any. I see no reason. And it is better not to take steps. They are so often called false."

"The evening is too much of a success," said Merton. "I must appeal to you, Aunt Penelope. A great-aunt is a safe character. Will you give Hetty your protection? Mine is not enough."

Penelope and Hetty turned to each other, the former at a loss for words, the latter at none.

The evening moved to its end. Alfred and his sister took their leave. When Merton returned from taking Hetty home, Galleon was standing in the hall.

"May I add my congratulations, sir?"

"You may. I am in a mood to expect them. I feel they are earned."

"May I also be glad of the accompanying circumstances, sir?"

"You may. I am glad of them myself. They will mean more ease."

"Complete ease I imagine, sir," said Galleon, smiling. "There will be no call for anything else."

"My work may improve, when I have no sense of urgency."

"Or be discontinued, sir," said Galleon, in an almost roguish tone.

"You would hardly expect me to do nothing."

"Well, sir, if there is no need of anything."

"Would you like to do nothing yourself?"

"Well, sir, I appreciate my occasional leisure. Nothing further is in question."

"But you would not like leisure and nothing else?"

"Well, sir, my life being of the opposite nature, I have no means of judging. I sometimes wish the duties were intermittent."

"As mine are? I have to wait on the mood. It must be so with my kind of work."

"It is not with mine, sir. Mood is not taken into account. It might lead to inconvenience."

"I believe you think writing is not real work."

"Well, sir, there is no great resemblance."

"It is not like digging potatoes?"

"No, sir, or like the manual duties of a house."

"Well, that is something."

"Yes, sir, it is in its favour."

"There is something I have not dared to tell you, Galleon," said Reuben.

"Oh, the attempt at schoolmastering, sir. It is a passing phase."

"Suppose it is a lasting one?"

"There is hardly any likelihood, sir."

"It is little better than writing?" said Salomon.

"Well, sir, hardly as good," said Galleon, in a serious tone. "In writing you are master of yourself, and there are no contacts."

"We ought to love our pupils," said Reuben.

"It is our neighbours, sir. The term is hardly inclusive."

74

"So our pupils are not neighbours?"

"Well, if their attitude was neighbourly, sir! But I gather it is not the case."

"But we are supposed to love our enemies."

"Well, if that is the ground, sir."

"Their attitude does present problems."

"Well, you will not have to solve them, sir."

"Why not? I have no share in my brother's prosperity."

"And prosperity need not end all human effort," said Merton.

"It tends to end a good deal, sir. It is often its object."

"I suppose another side of us can assert itself."

"Our better nature, sir? There is not always any need of it. In which case it is not resorted to."

"There is surely need of yours, Galleon," said Salomon.

"Well, sir, my life consisting of service to others, it must at one time have asserted itself once for all."

"But you do not remember it?"

"There is no point in recalling it, sir. It was not to my advantage."

"You did not really wish to live for others?"

"Well, sir, it was perhaps as far as I could go in living for myself. It could not be to any great length."

"You don't enjoy a glow of righteousness?"

"I am not subject to glows, sir. There is need of something to give rise to them."

"I believe I could be," said Reuben. "And I suppose Merton is at the moment."

"It is true," said his brother. "And the moment foreshadows a life."

"Here is a man we have not known," said Salomon.

"You are simple in your idea of me. Have you no depths yourself?"

"Yes, I have them myself."

"Then you have a weak imagination."

"Well, you need me to have such a strong one."

"One would think nothing had ever happened to you."

"Well, nothing ever has," said Salomon.

"And this has made you realise it?"

"It may have brought it home to me. And I am affected by the change in your life."

"And you would like a change in your own?"

"Well, I think I have become unfit for it," said Salomon.

CHAPTER VII

"What is it, Merton, my son? You have something on your mind? You will not hide it from your mother. Tell her what it is."

"I can tell the assembled family. Indeed I was about to. I will tell you first, if you will find it an advantage. I am not going to be married."

"Not going to? No, it is not true. It is simply some passing trouble."

"There are troubles that do not pass. You are fortunate not to have found it."

"Come, tell us, my boy," said Hereward. "If it is nothing, let it be so. If it is not, say what it is. We may be of help."

"That is often thought and said. People over-estimate their powers. Yours are great, if you can help this. You can hardly undo what is past."

"Come, say a little more," said Sir Michael. "It seems such an unlikely thing. The girl would not be at a difference with anyone. We already know it."

"I know it too. There is reason. That is what it is, or has been. How you are in the dark!"

"Well, shed some light," said his father. "You need not leave us in it. Let us look at the trouble with you."

"I will shed it fully. Perhaps you will be dazzled by it. Hetty is going to have a child. And it is not mine."

"Oh, no, it is not possible," said Ada. "There is some mistake. And of course it could not be yours."

"It is not. It is what I said. In your sense it could not be. I do not know whose it is. I am never to know."

There was a silence.

"It is sad news, my son," said Hereward, with his eyes

down. "Sad for you and all of us. Your trouble is your father's."

"Well, I would not have believed it," said Sir Michael. "I hardly believe it now. I don't know what to say."

"It seems to be the case with most of you," said Merton. "And I can't be of any help."

"You know what we feel," said Salomon. "You do not want our words. Have you broken off everything?"

"Well, it has come to an end."

"Is she to marry the other man?" said Reuben.

"No, she is not. He is married. That is all I know."

"This will not break up his marriage?"

"No, there seems to be no thought of it."

"What will be the future of the child?"

"I do not know. It is not my concern. When I knew the truth, it ended things between us."

"You are sure?" said Zillah. "That it ended them for ever? Say the truth to yourself and to us. Have you lost your feeling for her?"

There was a pause.

"Such a feeling does not die at once, or ever die. I need say no more."

Hereward was silent, his head bent as if in thought.

"What will her future be?" said Salomon. "We are forced to question you. You are not forced to answer."

"I am not able to. I do not know. It must be what she can make it. I hope it will not go hard with her."

"It seems it must," said Zillah, pausing after her words. "If she gave up the child, and the trouble was concealed, would you forget it and marry her? Would it be for the happiness of both?"

Hereward raised his eyes.

"I hardly know. It will be months before the child is born. And how could she give it up?"

"It could be adopted. The way is not hard. And perhaps she need not lose sight of it."

"You will help us, Zillah, if anyone can," said Hereward.

"I had not thought of it," said Merton. "And neither has she. I don't know how I feel about it."

"You hardly can, my son. You must take your time. We must have long thoughts in youth. The decision would shape your life."

"If I made it, I should mean it to. It would be the reason of it."

There was a pause.

"Have you not made it?" said Hereward gently, bending towards him.

"I have, Father. There can only be one. I can make no other."

"You are sure, Merton? Sure in your heart? Sure for the years of your life?"

"I am, Father. I have no doubt. I see I could have none."

"Then it is the best one," said Hereward. "There could be and might be others. But it is the best."

"It is mine," said Merton, lifting his head. "I hope we can do as has been said. Then things would be, as far as they could be, as they would have been."

"It is true," said his father. "And in a way and in the end they may be more."

"It is a great difference. It is another path. But it is one I can tread. I see it plain before me. It is no longer blank and dark. And I should be willing to give. I am taking much. And I am glad to be taking it. It will give her something on her side."

"You think and speak as yourself, my son," said Hereward.

"It is not unusual to adopt a child," said Ada. "We have spoken of it ourselves. You remember, Hereward, a few days ago. We said how we should like to have a child in the house again, and almost thought of adopting one. I don't mean we could adopt this child, of course."

"No, that could hardly be our choice," said Hereward, gravely.

"Why could it not?" said Sir Michael. "I see no

reason against it. It would give you a child whose parentage you knew, and keep Hetty's child under her eyes. There seems a great deal to be said for it."

"There is something," said Zillah, after a pause. "Merton would want to do everything for Hetty, if he did anything. It can only be everything or nothing, as he has really said. And it would give him a wife who was grateful to him, and at peace herself. And the secret could be kept."

"Would it be?" said Salomon.

"Yes, yes, of course," said his grandfather. "It could be all but forgotten. We should all do our part. We need scarcely say it."

"No, we could hardly fail in a trust like that," said Hereward. "But it is a serious and sudden idea. I don't know what to say. Any talk of adopting a child was casual. I only half-remember it. It was a passing thought."

"You agreed with me," said Ada. "I believe you gave me the idea. If you were casual, you were serious. You meant what you said."

"I am sure I did, if it fell in with a wish of yours. But words are only words in such a case. They must be taken as nothing more."

"Do we know anything about the child's father?" said Zillah.

"Enough," said Merton. "Hetty has not been silent. He is a man of a high mental type and of our own class and kind. More I am never to know. I shall not seek to. I have seen it as the final word."

"You are right to accept it," said Hereward. "It gives your course its meaning. You will be right never to question it. I feel you will be right, my son."

"It would be a good work," said Sir Michael. "There could not be a better. It is one I should respect, that I should regard with sympathy and interest. I should respect the feeling that led to it. And I speak in a serious spirit."

"I do not speak at all," said Joanna. "I am taken by surprise. You must all be people of the world, never at a loss."

"What do our sons say?" said Ada. "How do they see the idea? Are they enough ashamed of growing up to make their parents this amends?"

"Would not this child grow up?" said Salomon. "What you need is one who would not. You would suffer the same thing."

"Oh, it would take a long time. We need not think of it."

"No, we are in our later years," said Hereward. "This would take us towards our last ones. There need be no trouble there."

"I feel that light has broken," said Merton. "I will say once that I should be grateful."

"And I will say once that that settles it," said Hereward. "That and your mother's wish."

"How strange that we thought of adopting a child just at this time!" said Ada.

"The three young men in front of you are there all the time. One extreme suggests another."

"Well, it will all work out," said Sir Michael. "She will leave us for a while, and return as if nothing had happened. And they will marry, as if nothing had. And no one will connect the adoption with anything. And we must cease to do so."

"Mamma, have we asked your permission to have the child?" said Ada.

"I don't know," said Joanna. "I daresay you can tell me. But a noble course of action needs no permission. Only admiration. And that I give."

"We must see it as an ordinary course," said Hereward. "Nothing else need be thought or said. Anyone can adopt a child. We all know cases of it."

"The plan seems to have made itself," said Reuben. "We can leave it to develop in its own way."

"What do you think of it, Salomon?" said Zillah.

"Well, I feel we are moving over rather deep waters. But it is out of our hands, as Reuben said."

"It is Hereward who will benefit the most," said Ada. "We can foresee the success of the plan in his case."

"Well, childhood makes a great appeal to me. I have always been alive to its charm. It is a mark of the mature, worldly man, and calls for no surprise."

"Now there is a question, Hereward. Are my father and aunt to know the truth? We must make our decision and hold to it."

"They know it," said Merton. "I have told them. I asked if anyone else should know. And they said I should not face it alone. And I see they were right."

"Dear Father and Aunt Penelope! I feel they could not be wrong. I honour them equally. I have come to do so. It is good to find my son depending on them."

"I have found I can depend on you all, Mother."

"You must depend on no one else," said Hereward, gravely. "See that you do not forget."

"My boy, may your grandfather say once how he feels for you?" said Sir Michael.

"There is no need, Grandpa. You have shown it."

"And now must show it in another way," said Hereward.

"Now I am going to say whom I feel for," said Ada. "It may be unexpected, but I will say it. I often have a sudden feeling that is just my own. I feel for Hetty; for what lies before her; for having to face us with our knowledge; for feeling she must take so much, when she herself has failed. Merton is beyond pity, with the generous part. And that his mother feels for him need not be said."

"Perhaps none of it need have been," said Hereward, gently. "For the reason that his mother felt for him."

"Now here is our recurring difference. I do not believe in hiding what we feel. It means that no one knows we feel it. I will say it again. I feel for Hetty. A sense of guilt is no help with its consequences. And we all do wrong."

"And only the ordinary kind that does not add to us," said Joanna. "It hardly earns us any feeling. It is really expected of us. We might almost as well do right."

"Ah, the poor girl, we all pity her," said Sir Michael. "I quite dread meeting her in a way. I shall be ill at ease, as if I had done something myself."

"Well, perhaps you have, by not doing anything," said Reuben.

"There should be no trouble," said Zillah. "The moment will come and go. She will know what is being done for her, and will do her best."

CHAPTER VIII

Hᴇᴛᴛʏ ᴄᴏᴜʟᴅ ᴅᴏ no more than this. She entered in her ordinary way, looked once into everyone's face, and although more silent than usual, betrayed nothing. She seemed to control what she felt by holding herself from knowing that she felt it. She was, as always, appreciative of everyone, and by listening with especial attention saved herself from the need to speak.

The need fell on other people.

"Well, we are all together," said Sir Michael. "Just as we shall be in the end. It brings the future near to us. And it is not so far away."

"Grandpa knew he would be ill at ease," said Reuben. "He should have been prepared. Let someone talk about the weather."

"The gales never cease," said Merton. "They are doing harm to the trees. I hear more than one is down."

"The elements are against us," said his father. "Just when we want them in our favour. I mean, we all know people with journeys before them. I can think of several."

"He can think of one," said Reuben. "But he need not say so."

"An elm came down near a cottage," said Salomon, "and startled the cottager's wife."

"Yes, poor woman, she is expecting a child," said Sir Michael. "It is not the time for shocks. We must hope for better things ourselves. I mean I do for any friends of mine."

"It is said to be difficult to give our real meaning," said Joanna to her grandsons. "But I don't think it can be."

"The weather has failed us," said Salomon. "We are

84

supposed always to talk about it. And it does seem a suggestive subject. But I never will again."

"Never will do what?" said Ada.

"Talk of the weather, Mother. It is unworthy of me."

"Well, I don't know," said Sir Michael. "It can be a help when other subjects are forbidden—fail us in some way. It is awkward when there is a hush, and you could hear a pin drop, and everyone waits for someone else to speak, and no one does."

"What harm is there in hearing a pin drop?" said Joanna. "And there is little danger of it. When a pin is needed, no one ever has one."

"I have seen Hetty's house, Merton," said Hereward. "And I am as pleased with it as you can be. But the men can't begin to work on it yet. So much harm has been done by the gales."

"Well, there is no hurry now," said Sir Michael. "That is, they will do it in their time."

"We can do nothing," said Reuben. "We must just bear it."

"Just bear what?" said Ada. "Speak so that we can hear."

"We have countenanced the habit of whispering," said Hereward. "And now can hardly complain of it."

"There is no reason for it," said Sir Michael. "We should never seem to be covering anything up. It might give a wrong impression."

"It is more likely to give a right one," said Hereward, smiling at his sons. "The same as not covering it up."

"Father surprises me," said Reuben. "He is simply trying to help. He almost reminds me of myself. Can it be the simplicity of greatness?"

"I could almost think so," said Merton. "I have nothing but the truth to suffer. Many people despise the unfortunate, and hardly hide it. He does emerge as a man by himself."

"I wish you would include your mother in your talk," said Ada. "Who is man by himself?"

"Father," said Salomon. "We were speaking in his praise."

"What were you saying about him? Hereward, come and hear your sons' description of you."

"I spoke in praise," said Reuben.

"So did I," said Merton.

"I would have," said Salomon. "But the other two forestalled me."

"It is enough, my sons," said Hereward, in a moved tone. "Few fathers hear as much. I am content."

"Well, that is true," said Sir Michael. "Some would be wiser not to hear at all. When I think of the things I said about my father! But he did not hear them. So it was another matter."

"Your sons did not mean you to know what they said, Hereward," said Ada, moving forward. "It was the outcome of their real feeling. Dear boys, how fortunate we are!"

"And they are!" said Sir Michael. "There is the other side."

"Well, I have not kept apart from them," said Hereward. "I have tried to see things through their eyes. It has helped them to see them through mine. It has given us a shared vision."

The evening came to its end. Its minutes had been separate and slow. The hour felt later than it was, and put the scene into the past. Hetty left the house with Merton as simply as she had entered it. Alfred and Penelope entered as they left it. And the future took its meaning and its shape.

"Well, I am relieved," said Reuben. "Merton is not here to know. I have seen the depths, and should hardly have known they were deep. I feel I should be grateful."

"We must feel there is someone else who might be that," said Penelope.

"Poor little Hetty?" said Sir Michael. "Well, I have no doubt that she is. She had her own way of showing it.

She faced us bravely. I felt an admiration for her. I don't deny it."

"There might have been other feelings. It seems there is something in her that prevents them."

"There is. I felt it. I was alive to it from the first. I felt my heart turn over, when I saw her walk up to the cannon's mouth. I asked myself if I should have been equal to it. And I told myself I should not. I make no secret of it."

"I make most of what I tell myself, a secret," said Reuben.

"Many of us do," said Penelope. "We don't show too much of what is in us. There is an example of it in Hetty's case."

"Ah, your strong moral sense is in our way, Aunt Penelope," said Ada. "But your natural generosity will assert itself. We do not fear."

"When we talk of self-exposure, we do mean something derogatory," said Salomon. "It does not occur to us that it could be to anyone's credit. And as it is usually unconscious, I suppose it would not."

"How much of himself does Grandpa expose?" said Reuben.

"More than most people," said Salomon. "I think almost the whole."

"And Father?"

"I don't think much."

"Aunt Penelope?"

"More than she means to. But nothing to consider."

"Mother?"

"A great deal. She has less to be ashamed of."

"Grandma?"

"No one could say. Grandpa Merton what he must. Aunt Zillah almost nothing. The three of us as much as we dare. Galleon most of himself, as he sees no fault to be found in it."

"Some people suppress their better selves," said Sir Michael. "It is a known thing."

"Then they must make it known," said Salomon.

"You would think they would feel pride in their own goodness."

"They do," said Joanna. "So much pride that they cannot face it. And feel no one else will be able to."

"Could real goodness cause too much pride?" said Salomon. "An instance of it amazes me, or would, if I could think of one."

"Father's adoption of Hetty's child?" said Reuben, in a lower tone. "Wise or not, does it serve you?"

"Well, it does enlarge him for me."

"Is there any idea what the child's name is to be?"

"Zillah!" said Hereward. "A name that carries so much for me. My mother and wife would understand."

"Is the child to be a girl?" said Reuben.

"Yes," said his father, smiling. "I have three sons."

"And if it is a boy?"

"Hereward," said Ada. "So as to be a real son. We could call it something else."

"Is there anything to know about a child?" said Penelope.

"Oh, Aunt Penelope, a moment. Thereby hangs a tale. But this question of the name is a part of the same matter. I should have thought my own had the strongest claim, and should be inclined to assert it. But I know what it is to be called by it. So we will postpone the answer."

"Don't you like your name?" said Alfred.

"Father, how could anyone like it?"

"It was my mother's name," said her father, disposing of any objection to it.

"And does that make it the best name for anyone else?"

"It gives it a reason and a background. If you like, an excuse."

"Well, I am glad it has the last. It needs it."

"It does not need one to me."

"Well, tell Father and Aunt Penelope our plan, Hereward. Let them know the pleasant side of the matter as well as the other. 'It is an ill wind—' as we feel. I wonder what they will say to it."

"I think it can wait for the moment. It will emerge in its time."

"Let the time be now. There is no virtue in mere delay. I want them to know it. I feel a wish to share it with everyone."

"It is rather too much your own affair for that. But do as you will. It is because of you that the plan is made. Tell them yourself. Your own words will be best."

"Well, you know the dark side of the story, Father. Now hear the one that helps us to accept it. It is the moment to speak of it, as Merton is not here. It is clear that Hetty's child must be adopted. That conclusion came about of itself. Indeed it was foregone. Well, who do you think the parents are to be? You will hardly guess."

"Then do not expect us to," said Alfred. "It would lead to nothing."

"Well, I will give you your chance, Father."

"No, it is out of my sphere. I deal in certainties. It is not you and Hereward, of course?"

"Now why *of course*? And why should it not be? *Of course* it is. It will fill a gap in our lives. We have wished for a child in the house. It is so long since we had one."

"The last might be said of many of us. Of most of us after a time."

"I hardly knew my own heart," said Hereward, "and had to be informed of it. But I want what Ada wants. And I am a child-lover, as you know. It may work out well."

"You could have adopted a child at any time. This trouble can hardly have caused the wish."

"It has made us realise it," said Ada. "And it was not a new one. We had spoken of it. The plan will serve both our son and ourselves. What is there against it?"

"Nothing in itself. But surely there are other things.

It brings the matter too near for something that is to be concealed."

"Oh, we shall forget what lies behind it. We shall impose that condition on ourselves. We shall just adopt a child in the ordinary way. We might have done so at any time, as you said."

"As I have also said, it keeps it too close to everyone. Too close to you too, too close to your son and his wife."

"Oh, they know we are doing it for their sakes. They will think out their course and follow it. There is no danger there."

"Why is it for Merton's sake? How does it serve him?"

"By serving Hetty. By ensuring her peace of mind. His one wish is to be of help to her. And so of help to himself."

"You may soon be having your own grandchildren."

"But not a child in our own home. The grandchildren would be apart from us. We should be without a child ourselves."

"Well, it is true," said Hereward.

"You may come to feel a bias towards your own descendants. Will it be easy to keep a balance?"

"Yes, quite easy. Or quite possible. We shall make our resolves and hold to them. Indeed they are made. Now have I to refute any more objections? If so, let me hear them. I am ready."

"Ada has made up her mind," said Hereward. "And she is true to herself, and so cannot be false to any man. We need not doubt her. I have learned that I never need."

There was a pause.

"We are not to know who the father is?" said Alfred, relinquishing his stand.

"Not now or ever. Merton is never to know. It is the final decision, and may be the best."

"The father is responsible for the child's support."

"Oh, well, well," said Herward, moving his hand.

"That is as it may be. It is by the way. I am glad to give Ada what she needed. I had not realised her feeling. But for this I might never have done so. It has come about as she said."

"So you will never know the child's heredity?"

"We know enough. There is no need to know more."

"What do you know? You must forgive my pursuit of the truth. I am Ada's father and must question what lies before her."

"I will answer as I can. On one side you know what we do. On the other, the father is a man of our own class and kind. As I said, it is enough."

"He has hardly been true to either. And does he not know his obligations?"

"He has fallen in with our wishes and given us his trust."

"Through Hetty you mean?"

"It could be through no one else. But question me no further. I can say no more."

"We want to do everything for the child ourselves," said Ada. "So as to feel it is our own, and separate from our grandchildren. Doing all you can for someone is known to create a strong feeling."

"Well, it is a way of putting what you want, into your life," said Alfred, smiling. "And you might have a worse. You might indeed, my dear. It is a good scheme in some senses, a generous one in all. May all go well with it."

"Well, I am glad to have an approving word from you at last, Father. I wondered if I should ever hear one again. I do think the scheme has things to recommend it, and things not quite to be despised. Aunt Penelope, you say nothing."

"I say what your father said. As so often, our thought is the same. But I have a word of my own. What do Merton's brothers feel about it?"

"They have given their approval. It means they will do their part."

91

"It does," said Salomon to Reuben. "What will it prove to be? What an odd and sudden change! And what light it throws on everyone! What light especially on Merton! I did not know he was a noble man, great enough to forgive."

"Nor did I. I remember when he was strong enough not to have to."

"It was a different stage of life," said Sir Michael. "You have come to another."

"I have not," said Reuben. "I believe I should never forgive. And I am not sure that it is great. It seems to me rather humble."

"It could be both," said Ada. "There is humility in all greatness."

"There are other things," said Salomon. "Not always akin to humility."

"Great people always know how little they have achieved," said Joanna. "It does show how much they expected to."

"It is time for us to leave you," said Penelope. "We take away a great deal to think of."

"And do not let Father think of it in the wrong way," said Ada. "He will benefit much more, if he takes the right one. We are all going to benefit so much."

"Are we?" said Reuben, as his elders followed the guests. "Or are there troubles ahead? The wise ones feared it."

"We must avoid them," said Salomon. "It will become an unwritten law."

"What will become one?" said Hereward, glancing back.

"The avoidance of troubles arising from the new plan, Father."

"It must become a law," said Hereward, almost sternly. "And one that we never break. See that it is never broken."

Galleon entered as Hereward went on, wearing a face so expressionless as to suggest control of it.

"Oh, you have heard, Galleon!" said Salomon. "Oh, we ought to have thought of it."

"I did not hear, sir," said Galleon, specifying no further.

"I did not mean you could help it."

Galleon again did not hear.

"We know you will keep your own counsel."

"It is best as I have said, sir."

"You will forget anything you heard?"

"No, sir, it is best as I have said."

"It is," said Reuben. "We can only look up to you, Galleon. I suppose you look up to yourself."

"Well, I have my share of self-respect, sir," said Galleon, as he moved away.

"I can have none," said Salomon. "I almost gossiped with a dependant about our private family affairs! I have no respect for myself, and I have lost Galleon's. How his virtue has to be its own reward! When it is the only thing that deserves another."

"We will follow his example and forget everything," said Reuben. "But I feel we might be reminded."

CHAPTER IX

"Does Henry love Father?" said Hereward.

"No," said his adopted son.

"Oh, Henry loves good, kind Father," said Hereward, suggesting grounds for the feeling.

"No, Father love Henry," said the son, using the name that had come about through his own rendering of *Hereward*.

"Oh, why must we only love you?"

"Because," said Henry, looking at him with grave eyes.

"Don't you love anyone else?"

"Father and Nurse," said Henry, sitting up on Hereward's knee. "Always very much."

"Father does more for you than Nurse does."

"No," said Henry, surprised.

"When you are big, you will know it."

"Big now; very big boy."

"Yes, very big. You have lived nearly three years."

"Five," said Henry, erroneously. "Seven, five, eight."

"You will be more than that one day."

"A hundred," said Henry, with force.

"Even Father is not as much as that."

"Oh, no," said Henry, compassionately.

"How old do you think Father is?"

Henry raised his eyes in silence, unequal to the demand.

"It was Father who brought you a toy to-day."

"Broken," said Henry. "Poor horse!"

"Oh, how did that happen?"

"Break it," said Henry, illustrating the movement with his hands.

"Oh, that was not very wise."

"Very good boy," said Henry, in a precautionary tone.

"Let me see if I can do anything. Why, the horse is without a head."

"No," said Henry, putting the head and body together to remedy the position.

"You would not like your head to be apart from you."

Henry broke into mirth at the idea, and took his head in his hands as if to safeguard it.

"So you did not like the horse?"

"Love it," said Henry, stroking the head.

"You are not very kind to your toys."

"Not put them away," said Henry, in agreement.

"Not when Nurse tells you to?"

"She could spare herself the trouble," said Henry, reproducing more than the words.

"She does not make you do it?"

"No good when they are young. A waste of breath."

"Why, here is Mother coming. Show her how pleased you are to see her."

"Always see Father."

"Oh, you have the child, Hereward," said Ada. "What a difference he makes to you!"

"Do you?" said Hereward, putting his face against the boy's. "Ah, you make a difference."

"One, two, three," said Henry, as his grandparents and aunt appeared. "Poor Grandpa has a stick."

"Yes, poor Grandpa," said Sir Michael. "You would not like to walk with one."

"Yes," said Henry, holding out his hands.

"No, it is Grandpa's stick."

"No, Henry's," said Henry, getting off Hereward's knee and advancing to the stick with open purpose.

Sir Michael gave it up, and Henry walked about the room, imitating his use of it, and appearing to find it an employment that could not pall. When he caught his foot and fell, he waited to be picked up and resumed it.

"Give the stick to your big brother," said Salomon.

"Not big," said Henry, looking at him.

"Yes, we are bigger than you are."

"Men," said Henry, in a somehow baffled manner.

"You are right. We are not big for men."

"No," said Henry, smiling at the expression of his thought.

"What do you call your horse?" said Reuben, as Sir Michael retrieved the stick.

"Horse," said Henry, surprised.

"But hasn't it a name of its own?"

"Horsie," said Henry, after a pause.

"Isn't its real name *Dobbin*?"

"Yes," said Henry, smiling again.

"And what does Dobbin call you?"

"*Sir*," said Henry, laconically.

"Does anyone call you that?"

"Yes, the coachman and his boy."

"What do you call him?"

"Davis. Or Davis dear."

"Why don't you call him *sir*?"

"Not a coachman," said Henry. "But the boy does."

"Would you like to be his boy?"

"Yes," said Henry, rather unexpectedly.

"And would you call him *sir*?"

"Oh, yes."

"And what would you do?"

"Hold the reins and have a whip."

"You have them both," said Hereward, who had provided them in miniature.

"Very small," said Henry, incidentally.

"Mr. and Mrs. Merton Egerton," said Galleon at the door.

Henry alone of the company gave no sign.

"Here are brother Merton and sister Hetty come to see you," said Ada.

Henry did not disagree.

"And will you come soon to see us?" said Hetty, stooping towards him.

"No, not soon."

"But you want to see little Maud?"

"See you," said Henry, as if this duty should suffice.

"Maud talks as much as you do," said Merton. "And she says words of her own."

"Baby," said Henry, seeing this as a mark of the state.

"We must ask her to come to tea with you," said Joanna.

Henry turned and climbed on Joanna's knee, got down and returned with the horse, and settled himself with a portion in each hand.

"They both change with every day like flowers," said Hetty, looking at him.

"Maud is at the age when it is almost with the hours," said Joanna.

Henry turned and put his hand over her mouth.

"Not talk about Maud," he said.

"Oh, but why not?" said Ada. "We talk about you."

"Yes, talk about Henry."

"We talk and think about you both."

"Yes, think," said Henry, as if this did not matter.

"Maud is a dear little girl. She does everything her nurse tells her."

Henry looked up at Joanna with a light in his eyes.

"Naughty Maud," he said.

"Now you are making a joke," said Ada.

"Yes," said Henry, giggling in recognition of it.

"Well, who is this coming in?"

"Great-aunt Penelope," said Henry, glancing at the door. "And poor Grandpa Merton."

"Why is he poor?" said Joanna.

"Spectacles. Poor eyes! Oh, poor Grandpa Merton!"

"Would you like to wear the spectacles?"

"Yes," said Henry, doubtfully.

"Go and ask if you may try them on."

Henry did so, and walked about, wearing the glasses and laughing rather unnaturally. Then he suddenly threw them off and returned to Joanna.

"Oh, you might have broken them. What would Grandpa Merton have done then?"

"Not wear them," said Henry, stamping his foot. "Never wear them any more."

"They did not suit his sight," said Alfred. "The result of the lifetimes between us. He thinks they affect me as they do him. I had better have them back."

"No," said Henry, trying to intercept them. "Not wear them ever again."

"Grandpa Merton sees nicely with them," said Joanna.

"Oh, yes," said Henry, standing with tears in his eyes. "They make everything good for him."

"Yes," said Henry, finding her tone dependable and sighing with relief.

"He sees what you do," said Salomon. "And is just as happy as you are."

"Ring-a-ring-a-roses!" said Henry, struck by the idea of happiness.

The younger people accepted the prospect, and the rite began.

"Again," said Henry, as they rose from the ground.

It was repeated.

"Again," said Henry.

The door was opportunely opened and Nurse appeared.

"May Master Henry come now, ma'am?"

"Not *Master*," said Henry, with a wail.

"Come then, Nurse's little boy."

Henry put his hand in hers and turned to the door.

"Won't you say good-night to me?" said Hetty, whose eyes had followed him.

"Good-night, sister Hetty," said Henry, in a tone of quotation.

"And you will say good-night to Father," said Salomon, seeing the direction of another pair of eyes.

Henry suffered the observance, and Hereward lifted him and held him close. He disengaged himself to the point of comfort, and remained passive, awaiting release.

"The first shall be last, and the last first," said Salomon, looking at them. "Of all Father's infants I have been the least to him."

"The last, the child of my old age," said Hereward, almost to himself. "No other has been so much blood of my blood, so deeply derived from me. We go forward, a part of each other. We join the future and the past."

Hetty's eyes changed, and in a moment went to Merton, who had moved away. Reuben glanced at her and looked aside. Hereward continued in another tone.

"Henry's way of echoing and copying everyone gives him his own place to me. He seems to represent you all."

"I have noticed that about him," said Ada. "He gets little touches from each of them. He is young to observe so much."

"He is not always beyond his age," said Merton, brushing down his clothes.

"Nuts in May!" said Henry, seeing the movement and accepting its suggestion.

"No, no, you have had enough. You know how it will end," said Nurse, referring to the outbreak of violence by which the young signify exhaustion. "You must come upstairs."

"Horse," said Henry, in an acquiescent tone.

The parts were put into his hands, and he was led away.

"Now we can talk to Hetty and Merton," said Ada. "They will feel it hardly worth while to visit us."

"When a child is about, no one else's existence is recognised," said Merton. "I sometimes feel with Henry that Maud's might be ignored."

"You are looking tired, my son. Are you working too hard?"

"All day and part of the night," said Hetty. "He has never had such a spell."

"I have had a grim moment," said Merton. "I will say a word of myself. I never know why it is a sign of baseness. I collected and revised what I had written, to prepare it to see the light. And suddenly and finally consigned it to outer darkness. I face the world with an empty sheet, and feel it will be long before it is filled. It may be a forward step, but it feels like a backward one."

"Which it is not, my son," said Hereward. "It is a man's step forward. It takes a man's strength. I would have taken it myself, if there had been need. It makes a bond with your father."

"And I have my own good fortune. In a way I am doubly blessed. I appear to work for my wife, and I work to fulfil myself."

"I could envy you," said Reuben. "I find that independence as a state is over-praised."

"I do not agree," said Ada. "I should be proud of anyone belonging to me, who achieved it."

"Then you are proud of Father and me. I hope equally."

"Well, in proportion to yourselves, my son. And I am proud of the qualities that lead to it. It needs self-denial and courage."

"I said it was over-praised. But it is more so than I thought."

"Most people pretend to admire such qualities," said Merton. "What they really admire is the power to avoid them."

"They don't even pretend to in my case," said Hereward. "They are disturbed when they hear I put effort into my work. They want to feel it is spontaneous."

"Well, I think that is nice of them," said Reuben. "I can't think of a kinder feeling."

"I am ashamed of understanding it," said Joanna.

"Well, I understand it too," said Sir Michael. "To do that would be a mark of genius. And they would like to think he had it."

"They seem nicer and nicer," said Reuben.

"And no doubt they do think so. And I daresay he has. If they want the proof, his books give it."

"I agree that they are nice," said Salomon. "They

don't think that genius is an infinite capacity for taking pains. It is a grudging and heartless theory."

"And a false one," said Merton.

"Well, we ought to appreciate them," said Sir Michael. "They are Hereward's readers, and we can't have too many of them."

"His work would always create readers," said Zillah.

"Yes, of course. It has created me. I feel I now belong to them."

"I have not been created," said Joanna. "I enjoyed the books from the first. And I am not at all sure I enjoyed them for the wrong reasons."

"Well, I must go and work for the readers," said Hereward. "If it is a humble position, it is."

"And I must go and work to gain some," said Merton. "And it is a humble position."

"And we must go home," said Penelope. "It has been good to have an hour with you."

"And to us to have one with you, Aunt Penelope," said Ada. "You don't know what these flashes of you and Father mean to us. They hold all the echoes of the past for me. My girlhood and my sister seem to be carried in them."

"Well, your girlhood and motherhood are in the hours for us," said Alfred. "It is no wonder that we seek them."

The older people went with the guests to the hall, and Salomon and Reuben were alone.

"You heard, Salomon? I saw you heard. Hetty heard too, and Merton did not. Don't pretend you don't understand. We both know you do."

"Would it be best not to understand? Best to forget?"

"We shall not forget. No human being could. And we must speak of it. No one could be silent."

"Well, words may be a safeguard. It is the suppressed things that escape. 'Blood of my blood, so deeply derived from me'. It is a warning. We are Father's sons."

"Things fall into place," said Reuben. "There are a number to be explained."

"Yes. Father's sympathy with Hetty. The way he saw other people's feeling for her. His acceptance of the news of the child. His wish to adopt it, and his contriving to represent the wish as his wife's. I was struck by that at the time, but could not explain it. His caring for Henry more than his own grandchild. The touches in Henry supposed to be copied from us. What a story it is! It should not belong to real life."

"It would be better in a book. I am sure I wish it was in one."

"It would. It is a pity Merton cannot use it. It is hard to be the victim of it, when he might find it useful. And the light on the character of Father! It is a pity he cannot use him too. He may be short of material. His progress seems in doubt."

"Hetty must live on the edge of a precipice," said Reuben.

"She was prepared. And she keeps her foothold. Father is on it, and is growing unwary. He should be warned, and we cannot warn him. We are in peril."

"I suppose Mother has never suspected?"

"Why should she? We did not suspect. She would not think it possible. And in a sense it was not. A father's having that relation with his son's promised wife! What man would have come to it?"

"This one," said Reuben. "He yields to all his feelings. He does more; he fosters them. That is how he gets them on to paper. If he subdued them, they would lose their force. And releasing them sets them free in his life. I understand it all."

"You have great understanding. Take care that it does not betray you. And remember that other people are without it. If this came out, they would see it through their own eyes."

"How do you see it?" said Reuben.

"Through mine. I cannot help it. I should not have thought it of him. What man would of his father? I resent being forced to think it. It is not a lapse we can condone. If he was helpless, he should not have been. We are masters of ourselves."

"Perhaps he was not. He is not a man who would always be. He can be carried away. Think how he is affected by his books."

"This was actual life. He knew it for what it was. The truth is what it is. It must not escape. It proves what we think of it, that we fear it so much. And Mother and Merton do not know. Remember they do not. If they do, the guilt will be ours. And it is a guilt that no man should incur."

"Why, what a solemn pair!" said Hereward. "What serious matter is on foot?"

"Henry and his story," said Salomon. "You will not be surprised."

"No, he makes a strange appeal to me. There is wonder in every child. And in this one I find so much. I feel that my love for him will remain and grow, instead of changing to another, as with all of you. It may be so with a late child. And to me he is the last of my sons. It is strange that so great a good should arise from what might be called a wrong."

"It must be called one," said Salomon. "What else could we call it?"

"It might have been almost unconscious."

"What led up to it was not."

"Well, well, we will not judge," said Hereward, as he turned away.

"We can't all arrange for our wrong-doing not to be judged," said Salomon. "The weak point about it is the judgement."

"It is what there is to trouble us. We don't find anything else. Anyhow Father does not. And people feel a zest in judging. I am glad I never do wrong."

"I never do either. 'Not anything the world calls wrong.' And I think the world must know. Indeed we see it does. But if we cannot speak without referring to the matter, we are bound to betray it. I feel the deepest misgiving."

"And Father feels none. The danger is there. What has happened can happen again."

"The words may escape at any moment. They are on the edge of his mind. But are we quite sure of their meaning? Were they used in a literal sense? He has been fond of us all as children."

"He has," said Reuben. "And here is one of us."

A cry came from an upper floor, and the brothers' footsteps joined the others on their way to it.

Henry was sitting up in bed, looking small enough for any trouble to be large for him, and Nurse was standing, remonstrant and unruffled, at his side. He spoke in an accusing tone.

"Poor Grandpa Merton wear them! Hurt him very much."

"No, no, he is not wearing them now," said Ada.

"Yes, Henry see him. He always wear them. Oh, dear Grandpa Merton!"

"No, he left them behind," said Hereward, with a glance at his wife. "He will never wear them again."

"No?" said Henry, relaxing in a doubtful manner.

"There is a pair on the table in my room," said Hereward, in a rapid, incidental tone that eluded Henry. "Let someone fetch them."

This was done, and Henry looked at them in recognition.

"Yes," he said in relief.

"So that is all right," said Ada. "You can go to sleep."

Henry kept his eyes on the glasses.

"You don't want them, do you?" said Nurse.

"Yes," said Henry, holding out his hands.

"What will you do with them?" said Salomon.

"Not wear them. No. But very nice spectacles. Henry's."

"Look how well they suit me," said Reuben, putting them on.

"Yes," said Henry, smiling at the sight. "But Henry's spectacles. Grandpa Merton give them."

"Oh, are you sure that is true?" said Nurse.

Henry nodded without looking at her.

"Put them in their case," said Ada. "Then you can have them under your pillow."

Henry manipulated the case with interest and appreciation, laid it on the pillow by his own head, and prepared to sleep in its company, having an equal regard for its accommodation and his own.

"Henry is a person of a great compassion," said Salomon.

"He shows many qualities," said Hereward.

"He is a person of a great acquisitiveness," said Reuben.

"Not more than any other child," said Nurse.

"And of a great self-complacence."

"Not more than you were at his age. All children are alike."

"I wonder who thought of the innocence of childhood. It must have been a person of a great originality."

"But how innocent a child is, compared to ourselves!" said Hereward. "We have only to think to know it."

"It hardly needs thought," said Salomon.

"Well, well, we can hardly go through life without a stumble."

"We all do wrong, sir, it is true," said Nurse, accepting the current theory, though she was herself an exception to it.

"And the wrong is great more often than we know," said Ada.

"Well, if it was great, we should not know," said Salomon.

CHAPTER X

"I AM SURPRISED at myself," said Reuben. "I am just like everyone else. I am sure you will all be surprised. Of course I think you are all thinking about me. I said I was like everyone else."

"One moment, my boy," said Ada, who did the family carving and was engaged on it. "Let me hear when I can attend."

"You will not hear until you do. I take myself very seriously. I am exactly like everyone else."

"Well, what is it?" said his mother, with her eyes on a plate that Galleon was taking from her.

"I am treading in the usual steps, and thinking I am the only person who has done so."

"You yourself?" said Ada, in a different tone. "You are going to be married! Or you think you are. Another of you. And at your age!"

"It would not be unnatural, if it was all of them," said Hereward. "They are at the normal age."

"But it is me, Father. That is not natural. I am sure you can't think so. Anyhow no one will agree. You see that Mother does not."

"Well, I am glad," said Sir Michael. "I find it good news. I don't believe in postponing everything and prolonging youth until there is none of it left. I did not do it myself, and it has turned out as you see. Where would you all be, if I had? I congratulate you, my boy. I am glad to have lived to see the day."

"So am I," said Joanna. "I am sure we all are. That is what we do live for. To see days."

"I must know a little more before I am glad," said Ada. "Where did you meet her, my son?"

"At the natural place, the scene of my life. Where else should it be?"

"At the school? You met her there? She has not anything to do with it?"

"Yes, she has a minor position there. I·share the general view of that. We are all like everyone else."

"You want to rescue her from it," said Sir Michael. "It is another reason for marrying. I sympathise with you. It would be my own feeling."

"It hardly sounds quite what I wished for him," said Ada. "But I have not heard the whole."

"Well, I suppose it does not," said Reuben. "It would be a strange wish for a mother."

"Tell us everything, my son," said Hereward. "You know we are waiting to hear."

"I have told you most of it. And the rest you seem able to supply. But I need not keep anything from you. Her name is *Beatrice*, and she is called *Trissie*. She has nothing, and to me she is everything. It somehow sounds rather clever."

"It sounds as if cleverness might be needed," said Salomon.

"What a very nice name!" said Joanna. "Of course she would not have anything. *Beatrice* means 'blessed', and naturally blessed people would not. They would be ashamed to."

"And it is more blessed to give than to receive," said Reuben. "And she finds it is, and so would never have anything."

"Come, come, money is not everything," said Hereward. "It plays its part, and I am glad to have and use it. I may be able to help. Reuben may be thinking of it."

"I was not, Father. But I am glad if you were. I have no reluctance to be under an obligation. I should like to be under one. You know I am like everyone else."

"How good human beings must be!" said Joanna. "I don't think they have the credit of it."

"How long have you known her, my boy?" said Ada.

"Since she came to the school a year ago. We met on a common ground of grievances."

"But when they pass, your feeling may pass with them."

"They will not pass," said Joanna. "He spoke of grievances."

"What does she teach?" said Zillah.

"Something to the younger boys."

"Don't you know what it is?"

"I know what it is called. The name is *English*."

"What does she call it?"

"*English*. I said that was the name."

"Does not she know what it is?"

"No, or she would be teaching older boys."

"Are you serious, Reuben?" said Ada. "This is not a joke to us."

"Yes, I am. It is only the little way I have."

"Has she a little way too?" said Salomon.

"Yes, people will smile at the sight of us. We shall be such a quaint little pair."

"Well, I smile at the talk of you," said Sir Michael. "I am amused by it, whether I should be or not. And I think it will all turn out well. I have a feeling that it will. And my feelings are usually sound."

"My feelings are mixed," said Ada. "May it be the right thing for you, my son. When are we to meet your Trissie?"

"Next week. I have asked her to stay. You are right that she is mine. She did not want a single, great occasion. She felt an ordinary visit would be more in accordance with her."

"What does she mean?" said Sir Michael.

"You will soon know," said his grandson.

This was not to be wholly true. Trissie came in without embarrassment, and with a simple acceptance of what was to become her own. She was small and spare without being fragile, with light eyes, a pale, freckled skin, a small, alert nose, and an almost covert look of something that was akin to humour. A certain ease and confidence lay under a sub-dued exterior.

"Now you are to be my second daughter," said Here-ward. "I am in want of daughters, and grateful to my sons for providing them."

"I am glad I am to be the second. I am never first in anything."

"Oh, come, you are first to Reuben in everything," said Sir Michael.

"Yes, but he is a third himself. He would never be first either. Of course he is better than I am."

"You will be sorry to give up your work," said Zillah, after a pause.

"No, I shall be glad to. Before I am found out."

"Found out? In what way?"

"In not being equal to it. And so in being dishonourable in doing it."

"Why did you take it?" said Sir Michael. "I mean, how did you come to make the choice?"

"I had to do something. And there was nothing I could do. So there was no choice."

"Of course there was not," said Reuben. "It was the first thing we had in common. And it led us to see that we should have everything."

"Do you like the head master?" said Ada. "Reuben does not very much."

"No. I am afraid he will ask me how the boys are getting on."

"And can you not tell him?"

"Well, I can't say I don't see how they can be. He would only be surprised."

"You could make up something that would satisfy him," said Salomon.

"I think he would be able to tell. A schoolmaster would be so used to it."

"I suppose it is dreadful to work? I am the one of us who has never done it."

"Yes, it is," said Trissie, soberly.

"My son knows quite well what it is," said Hereward. "He does the work I should do, if I had the time."

"You do not call that work?" said Salomon to Trissie.

"Well, it is just looking after what is your own."

"You will have a house to look after, if you marry Reuben."

"Yes, and that will be the same."

"A poor thing but our own," said Reuben. "That is what you feel it will be. I have found it. That is what it is."

"I daresay no one else would want it," said Trissie. "But I always like what is mine. It isn't very nice when nothing is."

"Where is your home?" said Zillah.

"In a country village. My father is the clergyman. That is why I had to work."

"And you were busy in the parish as well?" said Sir Michael.

"Well, we did sometimes take things to the poor."

"That must be a pleasant thing to be able to do."

"Well, we really weren't able to. A clergyman has to do it, even when he isn't."

"Is your father pleased for you to marry?"

"Yes. It lessens his anxieties."

"I hope you don't mind all these questions," said Ada.

"No. Not if you don't mind the answers."

"We find them very interesting."

"I don't think they are," said Trissie.

"Have you ten brothers and sisters?" said Joanna.

"Well, I have a great many. How did you know?"

"Well, a clergyman in a country village! He does have eleven children. It comes in the great books. I think it is so dignified."

"It is not. It is different."

"And I am afraid your mother is dead?"

"She is. But how do you know? And why should she be?"

"She should not. It is sad that she is. It is in the books. All human life is in them."

"You must have great knowledge of that," said Sir Michael.

"No, we couldn't have any. Or only one kind."

"Well, you can support yourself," said Hereward. "That is a thing to be proud of."

"No one has been proud of it."

"I am sure your father must have been."

"No, he seemed rather ashamed that I had to."

"Well, I am proud of it for you."

"I don't think anyone else is."

"People are not proud of the right things."

"They are proud of the same ones. It doesn't seem they can all be wrong."

"Most of them are wrong about everything," said Merton.

"I don't think they are about this. Why should they be proud of what does no good to anyone?"

"Well, you look things straight in the face," said Hereward. "And there is something in what you say."

"There must be in what ordinary people say. They don't invent it, because there is no need."

"Reuben will live with a fount of wisdom."

"It is the kind I have had to get. It is only knowing what some people don't have to know."

"You are young to be married," said Sir Michael.

"I am nearly as old as Reuben. I know I shall never look mature. It does not matter now. It will be different when I am middle-aged."

"Well, he will not mind how you look. He likes you to look as you do. And he is not much to look at himself. I mean, it does not matter for a man. I have never found it did."

At this moment Henry entered, flushed and disturbed, followed by Nurse in a similar state.

"Naughty dog! Nurse run away. Henry did too."

"A dog ran after him, ma'am, and I had to follow them," said Nurse, in an incidental tone. "The young dog from the stables. It was only in play."

"Bark at Henry! Bite him!"

"No, no. You know he did not bite."

"He want to. Breathe at Henry. Look at Henry with his eyes."

"Bring the dog in here," said Salomon. "He must learn not to be afraid of it."

The dog entered in a friendly spirit, and Henry looked at it with a reverent expression.

"Dear, dear doggie! Wag his tail. Look very kind."

"Yes, dear doggie. Stroke him," said Nurse.

"No," said Henry, recoiling with his hands behind him.

"He does not want to bite any more than you do."

"Not want to," said Henry, in a shocked tone.

"You never bite, do you?" said Ada.

"Yes, poor Nurse! Only once. Never any more."

"Come and say how-do-you-do to sister Trissie."

"Not sister," said Henry, looking at her. "Come to see us."

"No, not sister yet," said Trissie.

"No," said Henry, nodding.

"Well, say how-do-you do?" said Nurse.

Henry looked up at Trissie, smiled and turned away.

"What a darling!" she said.

"Yes," said Henry, glancing back.

"You must come for your walk now," said Nurse.

"No," said Henry, going up to Joanna.

"I can't do anything. I am too afraid of Nurse."

Henry went on to Trissie, as someone less likely to have developed this attitude.

"Don't you like going for a walk?" she said. "I don't like it much."

"No," said Henry, sympathetically.

"Does walking make you tired?"

"No. Very big boy. Yes, very tired. Poor Nurse carry him."

"You are getting too heavy for that," said Ada.

"No, he is not heavy yet, poor little boy."

"He is like you," said Trissie to Salomon.

"He is an adopted child. But he copies us all. And that gives him a likeness."

"You are fond of children?" said Hereward to Trissie.

"Yes. But not of teaching them what I don't know myself."

"You felt you were sailing under false colours?"

"I don't think I have any true ones. Or I don't know what they are."

"Do you always speak the truth?"

"If I can. Then there is nothing to remember. And words mean something."

"Your true colours are clear to me. I shall be envious of Reuben."

"With all the people in your life?" said Trissie, looking round.

"I would not be without them. But there is something that is not there. Perhaps you will give it to me."

"I don't know what it is."

"You need not know. I can take it for myself. You may not understand what you give."

"Then it will not matter. It will have no meaning. But it must not be much, because of Reuben."

"It will not be much to you. If it is more to me, he will not mind."

CHAPTER XI

REUBEN DID NOT mind at first. But there came a time when he did; another when a sense of danger dawned and grew; and one when his feelings rose and carried him beyond himself.

He spoke to his father in front of everyone, as though meaning openness to ease the moment.

"Father, I must say a word to you."

"As many words as you please. The more, the merrier," said Hereward, who was in the mood of stirred emotions.

"You will not misunderstand me?"

"Why should I? You can be plain."

"Or read more than you must into what I say?"

"Why should I again? You are able to say what you mean."

"I must be. The time has come to say it. These hours alone with Trissie. They are so many, and they are somehow surreptitious. I feel they should cease."

"Oh, come, she is to be my daughter. I am her father as well as yours. I am to care for you both."

"You are to help us, and we are grateful. But it should not lead to anything further."

"It will add to our relation. That is as it must and should be."

"It should only add certain things. If it means others, I would rather not take the help."

"That is natural, as many men would not need it. As you do, you must accept it for your own sake and hers. And accept what must go with it."

"I did not know you wanted return. And return of this kind. I suppose I might have known."

"Say what you mean, if you mean it. There is no need to talk in riddles."

"I don't think I do to you."

"There is no reason to do so to anyone. Put your thought into words. I suppose you are not ashamed of it?"

"I am in a way. You are my father. My thought is not only on myself. There may be reason to be ashamed."

"You are young and ready to judge. I cannot help you there. You cannot help yourself. And you are the son of a man who lives in his imagination. If you are living for the moment in yours, it is no great wonder."

"Is there to be an end of what I mean, or of what I imagine? That is all I ask?"

"There can be no end. There is nothing to be ended. In your sense there has been nothing."

"Then I must make an end," said Reuben, in a deeper tone, seeming another and older man, as he lost his command of himself. "I have no choice but to force one. What has happened can happen again. What sort of man should I be, if I took the risk? There is Henry before my eyes. And before any other eyes that are not blind. The daily reminder of the truth, the daily proof of it. Do not think you have not betrayed yourself. You have done so all the time. And once it was in open words, in Salomon's hearing and mine. We had the proof of what we knew, and realised that we knew it. Yes, you can all hear me. I have betrayed the hidden thing. What was to remain hidden, what should have been hidden to the end. I was driven to it. I was helpless. And what have I betrayed? Only what you have known. You will find you have known it. And you will see the danger that I saw."

"There was no danger," said Trissie, with tears in her voice. "There was not anything. There would never have been. With him and me how could there be?"

"There was already something. My father was using his power. You were feeling it. You might not have withstood it. It had done its work before. Perhaps he cannot help it. He is not made up of strength. But does that lessen the danger? You must see it was too great. I could not face it. I would not. I could only force it to an end."

"Salomon, what have you to say?" said Hereward. "You hear what Reuben says."

"Father, it is a case for the truth. I cannot support both you and him. And the truth is on his side. It is true that your words betrayed you, that they were plain and meant one thing."

"Well, of course they betrayed me. They would always have done so. I have come to see Henry as my son. I have spoken of him in that way often and of set purpose. You will see there is nothing there. When I adopted a boy, I resolved to be his father. I have tried to keep the resolve. I hope I have not failed. I think we can say I have not. I may have kept it too well, or in too literal a sense. But to my mind that does not matter, and could hardly be."

"It could not," said Reuben. "But you have not kept another. You meant to be always on your guard, and it was a thing beyond yourself. It would have been beyond most of us. Always is a long word."

"A good many words are long," said Hereward, with a faint smile. "But the end of all words comes. I have forborne to hasten it. But I hope it has come."

"It has. And it is more than the end. The meaning and the memory remain. They will never be unsaid."

"Well, that would be a waste of time and energy and invention. And it is a shadowy edifice, built out of fancy. It would shatter at a touch."

"It is built out of truth and reason. It can be left to its life."

"Are these your own words, Reuben?" said Hereward, looking full at his son. "Their ring is not a true one. It is unlike you to be fluent and high-flown. Unlike you to use prepared speech. It is not hard to explain it. It is this moment in your life. It puts everything out of scale. Small things loom large, and chance words take another mean-

116

ing. That is what has happened to mine. And it is said that the words of genius hold more than the author meant. I am thought by some to use such words. It may be that it chanced then."

"These were not words of genius. I don't say that words of yours might not be. These were words of simple emotion, honest and deeply felt. In themselves they did you no discredit. But they betrayed the truth."

"I will not ask you what they were. It would give reign to your fluency, your fancy, whatever it is. It would lead you further astray."

" 'No other of my sons has seemed so much blood of my blood, so deeply derived from me'. They are not words of my fancy. They were not of yours. They came from your heart."

"Salomon, what is your real feeling about this?"

"What I have said, Father. I cannot unsay it. The truth has gone beyond disguise."

"Hetty!" said Merton, in a voice no more his own than Reuben's had been. "So this is why you were silent, why you would not acknowledge Henry's father, why you determined you never would. The man was my father. You and he fell to that. You were right not to tell me. It was better that I should not know. It would be better if I did not know now."

"I did not mean you to know. I thought you never would. But I am glad you do. It ends the thing that lay between us. And I did not feel it was falling. At the time it was something else. I looked up to your father. I still look up to him. You look up to him yourself, or you should. I thought his feeling was an honour. I still think it was. I forgot he was your father. To me he was simply himself. I was lost to everything, and I know he was too. And then I was glad for him to take the child, for it to have its true father. I was its mother, and I could not be. And it has turned out well. I think it was not a wrong thing. I think I did right to consent to it, right to be silent. You say you wish you had not known. And what else could I do? What would anyone have done? What would have come from revealing the truth? What has come from it now?"

Hetty's words had a sound of having been prepared, as though they were held in readiness in case of need.

"One thing has come," said Merton, looking away. "One that there must be, that cannot be gainsaid. I cannot see my father again. This is the last time that I speak of him as my father, to him as another man. Henceforth to the end of our lives there will be silence between us. My wife says she looks up to him. It may be that I never have. Something seemed to hold me from it. Something holds me now. It is a sad word to say and hear. And it cannot be unsaid."

Hereward turned away, as if accepting what was out of his power, and Salomon moved towards him.

"Father, is this wise? Is it a thing that should be? It would mean mystery and question. It might lead to the escape of the truth. It would bring trouble into our family life. It would help no one and harm us all. Is it not a case for thought?"

Hereward made a gesture towards Merton, as though the words should be for him.

"Merton, I need not say it again. You have heard it, and know its truth. The natural feelings of a moment are not those for a life. You have reason and judgement. I beg you to use both."

"Then I will use neither," said his brother, turning away. "I will neither think nor feel. I will keep my eyes from everything. I will forget I am alive. You speak of my reason. I will forget I ever had it. I must learn to have none. That is what you ask of me. I would ask it of no one. As you do so in the way you do, I will obey in the way I can. I have said what it is."

"Merton, I am grateful," said Hetty, going to his side. "I care for you more for this. I care in that way for no one else. The moment in the past is dead. I can hardly believe in the memory. I can't wish that Henry was not with us. There is no one here who can wish it. But that is all that is left."

"We know who Henry is," said Merton, almost to himself. "We thought we should never know. It seems strange that we thought it. He will come to think in his time. When he asks who he is, who will answer him?"

"The time is not yet," said Salomon. "Is not the present enough?"

"My wife, it is," said Sir Michael to Joanna. "It is much for us at our age. We must not judge, and will not; we must still look up to our son. This does not alter what he has been to us and done for us. But I wish we had not known. I wish I could have spared you at the end of your life."

"There was nothing to spare me. It is what I have thought. It is too late to say it now. It would be seen as wisdom after the event, and make people unkind. But not much wisdom was needed. I saw and heard and knew. And I am glad to be sure, and to see Henry as our grandson. And as I am glad, I will not complain, though I see that perhaps I should. I see how nicely you complain for me. But you need not talk of the end of my life. I like to feel I am in the middle of it."

"Am I utterly alone?" said Ada, standing apart. "Does anyone think of me, of my place in the grievous story? Is it only my son who has been wronged, and left to live under the wrong? I have to see the truth for myself, to face the difference. Henry has belonged to us all. Now he is Hereward's son and not mine. The same change goes through everything. This house is my home no longer. It has always held a life without foundation. I have felt the emptiness underneath. I forgave the trouble with my sister. But I cannot always forgive. It becomes a weakness and an indifference to wrong. And this wrong was deliberate and furtive, and the deception was to last my life. And further wrong was on the way. I cannot live in dishonour, with a husband I cannot trust. I will return to my father, to rectitude and strength, to a man who can rule himself. I feel I am under an alien roof. My younger sons have left it. My eldest must make his choice."

"I hardly can, Mother," said Salomon. "This house is at the root of my life. It is bound up with my being, with my boyhood, with all I have ever had. It is the scene of the only life I have known. I will be honest; of the life I have wearied of, but would not leave. My brothers have lives of their own. This is the whole of mine. The choice is made for me. Or rather I have no choice."

"Well, your mother believes in honesty," said Hereward, keeping his eyes from his son. "She will not find fault with that."

"I find none, Hereward. I see it is straight and clear. And I see its truth. And I can keep in touch with Salomon. You would not put trouble in the way. You would not fail us there."

"You will think again, Mother," said Salomon. "What will you lose, if you leave us? Your life with your husband and sons, your place as a wife, as a woman who has done well, ai..l won return. These things are not nothing to any honest woman, or in the eyes of any honest man. And in themselves they are much. You have lived with the wrong for years. It is no greater than it has been. What would you gain but loneliness and a sense of being revenged? Are these things worth so much to you, being the woman you are? We have seen what you would lose. Think of me and of your other sons. Think—I will say it—of my father. His weakness needs your strength. His kind of helplessness needs your help. This last threat shows his need. Will you not give it to him? Ask your father. We know his home is yours. But ask him if you do not need your own."

"What do you say to it, Father? They are plausible words. But is not their danger there?"

"They might be mine," said Alfred.

"But, Father, what of the wrong to me, and so to you? Is it nothing to you? Are you untouched by it?"

"I am touched to the heart. I am your father. But I have long known of this. When I have come, I have seen and heard what escaped those who lived with it. When I was once alive to the truth, it lay before my eyes. No one can be always on his guard. The moment when your sons heard incautious words, was not one by itself. I hoped it would not escape. I feared it would. It has, and we can only face it."

"Aunt Penelope, what do you say? I know you will speak the truth. I know that Father has spoken it. I must steer my way between you. Have you known what he thought?"

"No, he has been silent. I did not know. I have known only with you. When I knew, I felt at first with you. I saw myself in your place. And then I felt with your son, and then with your father. Their words convinced me. I feel they should convince you. It is a poor account of myself."

"No, it is an honest one. One that few people would have given. So you all advise me to accept the truth, and to begin my life again?"

"No, to go on with it," said Alfred. "There has been no change."

"There has been a hidden one. And there might have been another."

"My dear, it is all the same thing. Your husband has his powers and his weakness. You are faced with one; you are still dependent on the other. I am grieved and angry. I did not wholly like the marriage. But it is late to undo it; we know it is too late. For you own sake, for his, for your sons', for your father's, you must take it as it is."

"Well, I will be guided by you, Father. I have lived by your guidance and never found it fail. I will stay with my husband and my son. It may be the better thing."

"Do not stay for my sake," said Hereward. "Do

nothing that is not for your own. I will fall in with either course."

"I suppose it is for my own sake, Hereward. It is taking what is left. I will be honest; it is keeping what I have. There would be nothing in its place. And it is better for my sons. And I feel it is better for you, though you may not say it."

"I should not say what does not need to be said."

"And shall I do and say likewise?" said Merton, in a tone of self-mockery. "Am I also to retract my hasty words? 'I will try to be a son to you, Father. Better perhaps than I have been. If I had not failed you, you yourself might not have failed. Let us learn from each other'."

"I am glad, Merton," said Hereward, as if accepting the literal words. "I will not say more. Again it need not be said."

"Zillah, how much have you known?" said Ada. "Hereward keeps nothing from you."

"Nothing. He did not keep this."

"And you accepted and condoned it?"

"He is himself, as we are all ourselves. He too may have had to condone. He too may have wished for a difference."

"You mean I have not been the wife for him?"

"I mean you must accept him as he accepts you. The demand is the same on you both."

"To you that is fair," said Ada, sighing. "It would not be to everyone. It is not to me. What we are and what we do are separate things. We can control the one and not the other. I shall have to try to forget."

"It is not fair," said Alfred. "You have done your part. And Hereward has not done his. And you will not forget. But a wrong is better suffered as it is, than carried beyond itself. That you must suffer is no reason for suffering further."

"How wonderful everyone is!" said Joanna to her husband. "I did not know they were all like this. I know that some troubles bring out the best in people. But I should not have thought this was one of them. I suppose, when there is so much quality, anything does to bring it out. I am so proud of everyone."

"Well, I am proud of everyone but Hereward," said Sir Michael in a low tone. "I can't reconcile myself to this. I had had no thought of it. I am not a person who suspects such things. I can't understand the excuses made for him. Though of course as his father I am grateful."

"Oh, but isn't it better to be proud of him too? We should not like him to be left out. And a mother has to forgive everything. It has always been recognised."

"I suppose a father should too."

"I don't think it matters about a father. Anyhow there is no rule. Perhaps we only have rules that can be kept."

CHAPTER XII

Henry ran into the room and paused with his eyes on Trissie's face.

"Poor sister—!" he said, at a loss for the name. "Come to stay with us and then cry."

"I can't help it," she said, speaking to anyone who heard her. "It is all through me. You were happy, and you will never be again. And I have not done anything. I never have. I am not a person who could. When people are kind to me, it is because I am less than they are. I did not want to be. I wish I was not. How could I think it was anything more, when it has never been?"

Henry waited for her to pause, placed a doll on her lap, and went on to Hereward. He was not taken up as he expected, as his father was conscious about showing his feeling for him.

"Dear, dear doggie!" he said, looking round. "Not run after Henry any more."

"So you met the dog again?" said Ada.

"Oh, yes, met him."

"No, you know we did not," said Nurse. "You must say what is true."

"Oh, yes, always say it."

"You only thought about the dog?" said Hereward.

"Yes, think about him. And he think about Henry."

"What a nice doll it is!" said Trissie.

"It is mine, you know," said Henry, glancing back.

"Will you give it to me for Maud?" said Merton.

"Oh, yes, he will."

"Are you quite sure you don't want it?"

"New one," said Henry.

"Oh, you are a spoilt little boy," said Nurse.

"Yes, he is. Not Maud; just Henry."

"Well, you can buy a doll to-morrow," said Hereward, his voice seeming to assume a return to normal life.

"To-day," said his son.

"No, the shop is shut," said Nurse.

"No," said Henry, whose disregard of truth was equalled by his suspicion of it.

"It will be open in the morning."

"Very nice shop. Very large. Buy a train."

"No, no. You are to buy a doll."

"A kite," said Henry, with humour in his eyes.

"No, a doll. You must not be greedy."

"Oh, no. Give one to Maud."

"Will you give her the new one?" said Merton.

"No, Maud like this one better."

"Well, let me have it for her."

"No, one, two. Henry have them."

"So there is not one for Maud after all?"

"Yes, poor Maud!" said Henry, offering the doll.

"You had better seize the moment," said Hereward, smiling at Merton, and going to the door.

"Well, what a scene!" said Salomon to Reuben. "What power we had, that we thought we should not use! I suppose people always use it. The sense of having it leads to one end."

"I was driven to it. And no wrong is done. We were living over a morass. The surface was already broken. Uncle Alfred and Grandma knew."

"I can say nothing," said Merton. "There is nothing that can be said. What is unspeakable must be unspoken. It will be in the end. It is not that it throws Father off the heights. He was never on them to me. It has done something that will never be undone."

"But he is to return to the heights," said Reuben. "You are to find you have never liked him so well. You gave your own hint of it."

"And it is what happens when wrong-doers are exposed,"

said Salomon. "I always feel I should like them less. But it seems to be unusual."

"You must go, Aunt Penelope?" said Ada. "It has been a strange day for you. You will come in future with a new knowledge. You will know what lies under the surface of our life. Well, we shall talk with a full understanding. And Father will not carry hidden thoughts."

"It seems that a good deal of good has been done," said Joanna. "Of course we know that truth is best. But sometimes it hardly seems it would be. I am rather surprised that it is."

"You feel the moment is a light one, Grandma?" said Merton.

"What a word for a writer, Merton! Surely you know about the melancholy that underlies all humour."

"It now underlies everything for me. Nothing can be set apart."

"There may be little outward change," said Zillah. "We shall know what we do, and never mention it. The subject will protect itself."

"Then it is not like other subjects," said Joanna. "But then I suppose it is not. There would not be any subjects, if we had not developed the power of speech. They are not really natural!"

"It does not seem the word for this one," said Salomon. "And the guests will be gone and leave us with it. How will Father meet the occasion? He may be equal to it. He must have carried off a good many."

Hereward carried off this occasion by at once ignoring and accepting it. He joined in the talk as it arose, neither alluding to the disclosure nor avoiding what it involved, and as soon as it was natural, spoke of his work and left them.

Sir Michael had sat by himself, hardly glancing at his son, and speaking barely enough to avoid the effect of silence. He leaned back with an open sigh.

"Well, this is a relief. It is a chance to sort our thoughts.

We have to get used to the truth. I admit I find it much. I feel I shall never see Hereward without remembering it. And perhaps we ought not to forget. It is sad knowledge for his sons. And my Zillah has had to carry it alone. She could not turn to her father."

"Hereward and I shared it, Father, as we have shared everything."

"You were nearer to him than his wife," said Ada. "It was as it had to be. I suppose it is how it has always been."

"His wife was hardly the person to share this secret," said Salomon. "It was largely because of her, that it had to be one."

"I am a wronged wife," said Ada, almost musingly. "It is a strange thought. And that I accept it is stranger. I wonder how I shall feel to Hereward, how I shall manage our life together. It will be a test."

"Ah, you will be equal to it," said Sir Michael. "I have no doubt of you, my dear. I am as proud of my son's wife as I am of my son. She is as much above him in one way, as he may be above her in another. And her way may be the better. To me I admit it is. This is a grief to me. I can't deny it."

"Grandpa feels it more than anyone," said Reuben, resuming his usual tone. "He must be a very good man."

"Grandma has always known," said Salomon. "And she has not felt it at all. What a good thing she is not a very good woman!"

"I admire goodness," said Sir Michael. "I can't say I do not. I don't mean I am good myself. I admire it wherever I meet it. Hereward has been a good son to me. He has not failed his father. It is not for me to judge."

"It is for us all to judge this," said Reuben. "There must be some moral standard in human life."

"Standards seem to be based on the likelihood of their being violated," said Joanna. "I suppose my son is a man like other men. Though I am not sure that so many men are. You see your grandfather is not. I don't think there is such a thing as a woman like other women. Perhaps there are no other women. Or not enough of them to count."

"There is a child who may be like other children," said Merton. "But in this house it would not be believed."

"Let us go and look at him," said Trissie. "Children are so pretty when they are asleep. And he will grow into a boy and be different."

"And boys are so often awake," said Reuben. "And we have noticed the difference."

"I will go home," said Hetty. "Merton can follow me later."

"As you will," said her husband. "I shall not be very long."

"Hetty lives up to herself," said Joanna to Sir Michael. "She will not stand with Merton by Henry's bedside in Hereward's house."

"Ah, it was a natural feeling. It was a sensitive thought. I sympathise with it."

"So do I. How nice it is that we both have wide sympathies!"

When they reached Henry's room, a figure was in their path. Hereward was bending over the cot, his eyes on its occupant's face.

"Hush; he is asleep," he said.

"That is why we are here," said Salomon. "It is our object to view him in that state."

"Do not wake him, sir," said Nurse, whose instinct had brought her to the spot. "He is disturbed by any sound."

"What of the deep sleep of childhood?" said Reuben. "Is it another of the illusions about it."

It seemed that it might be, as Henry stirred and murmured.

"Henry. Not Maud. Just Henry."

"I might come to say it in the opposite way," said Ada to her husband. "Do I begin to feel it?"

Henry's eyes wavered over her face, and he made an effort to speak.

"Yes, yes, always just Henry," said Hereward.

"Oh, no, poor Maud!" said Henry, in a reproachful tone, and succumbed to the kind of sleep expected of him.

"He has held us together, Hereward," said Ada. "Will he now come between us?"

"No, you are yourself, and he is helpless. I will trust you, as I know I can. It is you who are proved worthy of trust."

Nurse moved away, as though as unconscious of their presence as they were of hers.

"Well, we have the hours before us," said Salomon, as they left the room. "We can't take refuge in sleep like Henry. And even then Father might come to look at us."

"Not at me," said Reuben. "It could only be at you. For Merton he must have the awkward feeling we have towards someone we have wronged. What has Merton to say to me? I meant to be silent to the grave. I was driven beyond myself."

"The truth was there," said his brother. "It has lain between my wife and me. The change is in my feeling to my father."

"What an hour he has lived!" said Salomon. "Could anyone have deserved it? His guilt exposed and discussed before him! And judgement and mercy meted out! To him, the head of the family, and destined to remain so! The way he did remain so showed the man he was."

"He had already shown us that," said Reuben. "I don't regret that I betrayed him. Why should I control myself? I am his son."

"Not wholly," said Hereward's voice behind them. "I may not always be master of myself. But I have never betrayed another man. Any other man's secret is safe with me. If you would not have my actions on your conscience, I would not have yours on mine. You may come to the first, as your life goes by. I shall not come to yours. That is my word on the matter. I shall say no more."

"But I shall," said Reuben. "Your secret was safe. It would have been safe to the end. But it was leading to another. That is my word. I too shall say no more. It is enough."

Hereward passed them in silence, and Salomon spoke in a low tone.

"It seems I can never be married. My wife would be in the house. I should live under a dangling sword."

"You would not," said Hereward, glancing back. "Your talking in that way shows you know it."

The brothers were silent until their father's door closed, and then went down to their mother.

"Well, you know it all, my sons. You knew when I did noi. In knowing your father's life you know your mother's. You see her wrongs and her forgiveness of them. And you do not see her exalted by either. I can put myself in your place. You feel she is humbled by both."

"Well, I did feel reluctant to take similar risks," said Reuben.

"You are not cast for a heroic part," said Salomon. "It is Mother who is."

"I did not know that anything could happen in a family," said Joanna. "I thought it was always outside them. And wild oats used to be sown in youth. Now it seems to be different."

"And they ought to be," said Sir Michael. "It is the right time for them. I mean, if they must be, it should be at that time. At the natural, excusable one. Or at any rate more excusable."

"You must not excuse it, Grandpa," said Reuben. "You must live up to yourself."

"Where is Trissie?" said Zillah. "I hope she is not still in trouble. She should be with us."

"She is in her room," said Reuben. "She will go to-morrow, and will not come again before our marriage. And I daresay not often after it. This must leave its trace. Father will never forgive me. And I am hardly inclined to set him the example."

"How you are meeting life!" said Joanna. "If I have not lived, I am glad I have not. I don't even like to see other people living. And they don't seem to like it very much."

"Ah, Joanna, you have a simple old husband," said Sir Michael. "He did not see what you did. He saw nothing. He took things to be what they seemed."

"It is what they generally are. It is conceited to say they are not. And it is really what they were."

"Well, the truth has come out," said Salomon. "And few of us are wiser, and no one better for it. Shall we have to treat Father in the same way? We should not dare not to. But is it a moral duty?"

"Yes, it is," said Sir Michael. "He is your father, and you owe him everything. You take from him more than you return. Nothing else can be said."

"Many men have secrets in their lives," said Zillah. "It is by chance that this one has escaped."

"It was its destiny," said Salomon. "Henry could only be its betrayal. And he will be the reminder of it. I wonder Father was not prepared. He knew the risk he took."

He paused, as Hereward stood on the threshold, upright and calm and in possession of himself.

"Yes, I knew the risk and faced it. I knew what I owed, and to whom I owed it. That debt will not soon be paid.

"You have all given your account of me. I will give you my account of myself. I am not afraid of it, and you need not be. I do not speak to hurt.

"I am a man of great powers, swift passions and a generous heart. You have met them all, benefited by most, suffered from some. You will not cease to benefit. You will not suffer again. I am an ageing man. My vigour fails. This last approach was a light thing.

"But I still have a word to say. I am a man, as not all men are. If I have lived a man's life, what other life should I have led? I have carried a man's burdens, given up a man's gains, done the work of men. It is my nature that enables me to do it. It is the force in me that carries me on. All force may at times go astray.

"I have cheered the homes of thousands. I have served our family home. I have judged easily, pardoned much, helped others to fulfil their lives. I will help them still. I will still understand and give. Would some men ask a return?

"I will ask nothing. I have never asked. I find no fault with what has been. But am I not too simply judged? Should a stumble be so hardly forgiven? I will leave it to you. My word is said. I shall not say it again."

The door closed on a silence.

"Suppose he did say it again!" said Reuben. "How would things be then?"

"Well, I suppose it is true," said Sir Michael. "There is truth in it, of course. But I can't go the whole length. I feel we should keep our human laws. I am carried away at the moment. But I can't alter myself."

"I am really carried away," said Joanna. "So I must alter myself. I am going to try to be worthy of Hereward. You see I am already trying. And I think you must feel I am succeeding."

"I may disturb you, my lady?" said Galleon at the door. "It is already later than usual."

This was true, as Galleon and Nurse had met and talked in the hall.

"Well, when something should be safe with me, Nurse, that is what it is."

"Silence is my watchword, Galleon. It is natural to me, my tendency being to reticence."

"I am myself a man of few words," said Galleon, sighing in remembrance of large numbers.

"And this might befall any gentleman. It is not a loss of dignity."

"When he addressed the family, Nurse, dignity was the word. I shivered as I heard."

"I should have done the same. A gentleman justifying himself! It is not a thing that should be."

"Well, he did not lower himself. It marks him as what he is. And the writing cannot alter it."

"No, he keeps above it. It is a call for quality. Few would be equal to it. And I cast no stone. As regards me he has not failed."

"Ah, well, you know your time of life, and so does he."

"You can hardly be aware of it, Galleon. You go beyond yourself. And you are light in your talk of those above you. To fall is not to condescend. And you should not broach the subjects. It does not sit well on you."

CHAPTER XIII

"I AM RESOLVED, Aunt Penelope," said Ada. "I have
made up my mind. I will not let my heart be troubled.
I will not let it be afraid. Whatever happens, I shall
have my sister. We shall bridge the gulf of years and
re-live youth. It will be as if the parting had not been.
The reason for it is dead. And if it is not, I will not see it.
I will keep above what is beneath me. I will pay the
price that must be paid. Who should have learned that
lesson, if not I? I look forward with an easy heart."

"There should be no danger," said Alfred. "The
memory will be a safeguard. And time has passed."

"It is true, Father. I will feel it is. We turn to you for
truth. I will take full joy in the reunion, in the future
that must hold so much of the past. My sister will be
with me. My sister who has lived in my thought, who
returns as a widow to my care. I envy you, Aunt Penelope.
I grudge you the task of preparing for her. For her and
the adopted daughter we are to see as her own. I long to be
making ready for them. But I respect your prior claim. We
shall all be with you to welcome her. My sons know her
only as a name. So much has been forbidden to us, and to
Hereward is still forbidden. To him it is a matter for
silence. But I can forget it and go forward. This my sister
was dead and is alive again, and was lost and is found. I
feel I could break into song."

"You have not fallen so far short," said Alfred,
smiling.

"Oh, Father, think what it is to me. Even more perhaps
than to you. I have watched her growth as I have watched
that of my sons. And now the years of our parting fade
away. They will never mean nothing. We shall not atone

for the loss. But I shall have something of what I might have had."

"Watching my growth has achieved as much as watching anything else," said Reuben.

"You should be grateful," said Salomon. "Only a mother would have done it. Most people express surprise when growth attracts their notice."

"Even my father forgot about mine," said Trissie. "Of course there wasn't much to remind him."

"Oh, forget yourselves and your growth," said Ada. "It is someone else who is in our minds to-day. Our growth can take care of itself. We can all see how much of it there was. In my case there was a good deal. But I have no thought to spare for it."

"You have words to spare, as we had," said Merton.

"Oh, I make no claim to be consistent. My mind is too full for me to watch my words. I shall not be in command of myself until the moment comes. If only the days would pass!"

The days did not fail, and the family gathered in Alfred's house to await the arrival. The meeting seemed to come and pass before they knew. It seemed there was something wanting, to which they hardly gave a name.

Emmeline greeted them without emotion, and with an ease that was more in accord with their memory than their mood. She was heavier and soberer, and her charm revealed itself at once as more intermittent and ordinary. Her eyes went often to her adopted daughter, and her thought seemed to be on her more than on herself.

"My sister!" said Ada. "After the years of thought and memory. How I have lived in this moment!"

"My daughter!" said Alfred. "The other words can be the same."

"Your niece, Aunt Penelope!" said Emmeline, smiling and passing to the third embrace.

"My sons!" said Ada. "Your nephews whom you have not seen."

"And my daughter!" said Emmeline. "For that is how you must see her. It is what she is to me."

"And will be to us," said Penelope. "You did wisely to choose a girl. Your father is rich in grandsons."

"She has always been needed. She came to me when I was alone. And my husband was glad to share her. We never felt we were childless. You will not think of me in that way."

The daughter came forward, a comely girl of about twenty-two, seeming rather mature for her age. She had pleasant, straight features, large, hazel eyes, and an expression at once amiable, confident and resolute. Emmeline was always aware of her, and when interest turned to her from herself, seemed to expect and wish it.

Hereward moved towards them and spoke for every ear.

"So we meet at last. With much to remember and forget. We can do both. It is a clear way."

"It is," said Emmeline. "And it is more. It is to be a new one."

"I am a minor figure on the occasion," said Sir Michael. "But as Ada's father-in-law I can feel a part of it."

"I feel it might be the same without me," said Joanna. "And I believe it would."

"I feel you are my relations as well as Ada's," said Emmeline. "As we are sisters, it seems to be natural. But there is so much to know about you all."

"I will give you my account," said Hereward. "I am still the slave of the pen. And still by some held to be its master."

"I am one of those," said Hetty. "And I am Merton's wife. That is all I need to say."

"There is that about Hereward's books," said Sir Michael. "They can be read by people of any age or kind. To my mind it is the truest strength."

"One of them could be read by Grandpa," said Reuben. "I saw it admitting of it."

"So did I," said Salomon. "And the true strength was Grandpa's."

"I am hardly a slave of the pen," said Merton. "That implies too much. But I remain its servant."

"I am a useful member of society," said Reuben. "I should hardly be a member, if I were not useful. And that may show it is not society."

"I am nothing but myself," said Salomon. "So that is enough about me. There can hardly be any more."

"So am I," said Viola. "And I feel it is quite enough. Why should we be more than ourselves?"

"I am the person who provides Viola," said Emmeline. "Nothing further can be asked of me."

"Oh, I belong to myself, Mother. But I am glad to be with you in your home."

"She will belong to someone else one day," said Sir Michael.

"Not any more than he will belong to me. Things will be equal between us."

"Now there is another meeting," said Ada. "Viola, here are your grandparents. I see my aunt as a sort of parent. She has filled the place."

"I make no bid for attention," said Alfred. "There are many stronger claimants."

"Oh, you are still our show specimen, Father. None of us can hold a candle to you, though Merton owes you a debt. I am happy to be like my mother, but the prize for looks was yours. She would have been the first to assign it to you."

"I did not ever wish her different."

"No, and you would not wish me so. We do not want change in the people we care for. It would mean they were not the same."

"I daresay it would," said Salomon.

"It might be the outcome," said Merton.

"Now do not sneer at your mother. Any chance word can be taken up like that. It is too obvious a line to follow. Now who is this come to see us?"

Henry entered the room by himself, having been

brought to the house by Nurse and left at the door. He kept looking back, as if at a loss without her, and paused to gaze at the newcomers.

"Now who are these dear people?" said Ada. "Can you guess?"

"Two," said Henry, finding the number unusual.

"Yes, Aunt Emmeline and Cousin Viola. Are you not pleased to see them?"

"Very nice house," said Henry, looking round.

"Nicer than ours?"

"Oh, yes it is."

"It is smaller," said Alfred.

"Yes, dear little house."

"You know it is not small," said Merton. "Did you walk to it or let Nurse carry you?"

"Yes, poor Nurse very tired. Henry read to her."

"What do you read."

"Little Bo-Peep," said Henry, incidentally.

"You know it by heart," said Merton. "You don't read from a book."

"Yes, have a book and read."

"Well, read to us out of this one."

Henry took the Bible and proceeded with his eyes on it.

> " 'Little Bo-Peep
> Has lost her sheep,
> And doesn't know where to find them.' "

> " 'Leave them alone,
> And they'll come home,
> Bringing their tails behind them,' "

said Merton, exposing the method.

"And does Nurse listen?" said Hereward, disregarding his second son.

"Yes. Not tired any more. Show her the picture."

"And what else do you read?"

> " 'Ride a cock horse
> To Banbury Cross,' "

said Henry, looking down with the negligence of modesty.

"Would you really like to read?" said Merton.

"No, he is too young yet."

"You know you can't read, don't you?"

"Oh, yes, he knows," said Henry, with the air of a conspirator.

"We don't want Maud to pretend to read. We will wait until she can."

"Yes, pretend," said Henry, as if accepting the word.

"She has forestalled us," said Hetty. "She pretends already."

"Oh, no, not pretend," said Henry, in a tone of disapproval.

"He is getting rather spoilt, Father," said Merton.

"No," said Henry.

"Do you know what it means?"

"No," said Henry, easily.

"I don't think you are spoilt," said Viola.

"No," said Henry, smiling into her face.

"Have you a message for Maud?" said Merton. "You love her, don't you?"

"No, her," said Henry, indicating Viola.

"I have no little boy," said Emmeline. "Only a girl."

Henry looked round for the latter.

"Here she is," said Emmeline, putting her hand on Viola's shoulder.

"No," said Henry. "Lady."

"I think it is long enough, ma'am," said Nurse at the door.

Henry turned and ran towards her, ignoring the farewells that followed him.

"You are honoured among women," said Salomon to

139

Viola. "And indeed among men. We all strive for Henry's favour."

"Were you glad when your father adopted him?"

"I was surprised. But I like a child in the house. My brothers are married and provided for."

"You could marry yourself, if you wished."

"I would only marry whom I wished. And another point of view is involved."

"Is it strange to have a famous father?"

"I am used to it. It has become a part of our life."

"You do not want to write yourself?"

"The question does not arise. I am not able to."

"If you were, would you try to write like your father?"

"Would anyone try to do anything like anyone else? If I produced anything, it would be my own. But my father's work looms large to us. We depend on it for much of what we have. We can only be grateful for it. And there are parts of it, that I can be proud that he has written."

"Does he know how you feel about it?"

"He has two sets of readers, the large and the small. He knows I belong to the second, and is not concerned. He sees his work with his own eyes."

"Both may be right in a way. The larger need not always be wrong."

"It contains many honest people. I am not going to pity it, if it includes you."

"What of your brother's work? Has he also two sets of readers?"

"He writes for one. And it remains small. His work has not so far found a place. Of course my father's always did. But it is easy to judge such things, and difficult to do them. I have no right to speak."

"It is such a change for me to be with a family like this."

"It is not to me. But something else is a change. Something I have imagined and given no name. I can hardly give it one now."

"There may be things that have no names."

"There are. They are outside the sphere of words. If you had lived in that sphere, as I have, you would know it. They have their life beyond them."

"What an earnest pair!" said Hereward. "Am I allowed to join?"

"You hardly can," said Viola. "The talk was about writers, and you would have to lead."

"What has Salomon been saying of his father? I dare to guess I was an example."

"That you have written things he is proud of."

"Oh, so I have a loyal son. I was not sure of it."

"How can he not have?" murmured Salomon for Viola's ears, as he moved away. "Things being as they are. He being as he is. His writing giving us what it does. I am what I have to be. I do what I must."

"So you are my adopted niece?" said Hereward. "We will forget the adoption and keep the rest. We will forget it all, and have something of our own. There is a word I have to say to you. I want to take the place of the father you have not had. You will let me try? My heart would be in it. And it could be between ourselves."

"I wish you would try. I wish you were my father. I have thought and asked about you. But my mother could not tell me much."

"And am I what you imagined?"

"I did not dare to go far, in case I imagined too much. But it might have been the whole. You are just what you ought to be.

"So I have been told. And I should be what people want. They want my books, and I put myself into them."

"And you are yourself out of them. And it is said that writers seldom are."

"Their energy is used. As mine would never be. I say it of myself, as it is true. It is a thing that puts me apart."

"One of the things. It is what you are."

"And what you should not be," said Ada's voice.

"Come and join the rest of us, and put all ideas of being apart out of your heads. Apart! Why should you be? Why should any of us? I have never had such a thought in my life. The wish must be father to it. Come and join your—betters I almost said—but I will say your equals. That should be enough for you."

"For me," said Viola. "But what about my Uncle Hereward?"

"Enough for him too. In ordinary life he takes the usual part. His position with his readers is different."

"It is," said Hereward. "I will not deny it."

"Then it can be with me," said Viola. "I am one of them."

"Well, so it can," said Sir Michael. "And he deserves that it should be. He has a right to anything that comes to him."

"Very little comes to us, that we have not a right to," said Zillah. "We can accept it all freely."

Hereward accepted what came, until a time when it was questioned. Some weeks later Salomon approached him, and spoke of the matter in a candid manner that suggested it was not a great one.

"Father, you will let me say a word? It is nothing of great significance. I am not suggesting that history is repeating itself. I know your feeling for Viola is fatherly and nothing more. It has been clear from the first. That is why you have not thought. But in a way you are trespassing again on a son's preserves. I will ask you to leave my path clear. You are too impressive a figure to be in the way."

"What do you mean? What is it you are saying? You don't mean you are in love with Viola?"

"What else should I mean? I should be taken to mean it. I tried to make it plain."

"You are not thinking of marrying her? No, you cannot be."

"Why not? I am in a position to marry. You have

said you wished I would, that it was time. What is there against it?"

"Oh, my poor boy!" said Hereward. "My poor boy!"

"Why, what is the trouble?"

"Now I am an unfortunate man," said Hereward, throwing up his hands. "Here I do my best for my family, work for them, bear with them, make no effort for myself! And I become a threat and a danger and a despoiler of their lives! You tell me to get out of your path. There is a word for a father's ears. What if I had not been in it? If I had left it clear, as you say? It is true that I have had my temptations, and that my life has kept them at hand. But what would have happened, if it had not been so? Where would you have been without me? Where would those who matter more than you, have been? Your mother and mine would have been thrust from their place. Would you have been able to help them? Or would you have turned to me? Answer me and answer me truly. What can I be but what I am? What could I have done but what I did?"

"Father, have done. Be plain. You have said nothing yet. I feel you can have nothing to say."

"Salomon, I speak to you as to another man. You have reached your full manhood. You know that your mother's sister left us in her youth. That a threat was seen in her remaining with me. My son, it was more than a threat. The consequence came. Neither she nor I betrayed it. We felt silence was best. She adopted the child and still said nothing. I provided for its needs, and still provide for them. I had my usual part. Viola does not know. It seemed better that she should not. But it was not better. Nothing has been. Everything has gone awry for me. I look for nothing else. But of course I was drawn to her. Of course I was in the path. Did I not see her in mine? You have my sympathy, Salomon. You deserve it indeed. But I ask for yours. And I ask something else. I can face no further exposure. I ask that there shall be none."

There was a pause.

"Viola should know," said Salomon, in an empty tone. "Anything else has danger. We see the danger that it holds. And she must see the difference in me. Her own feeling may not have gone far. She welcomed your presence in the path. Well, it is clear for you now."

"Do not be bitter, my son. I have been as helpless as you have. And my way is not clear, if this is to be known. It is not the word."

Salomon spoke in a more natural way.

"It should be known, Father. Viola has her claims. The knowledge may affect her future. She is my grandparents' true grand-daughter."

"My son, she is the child of your father and your mother's sister. She is your half-sister and more. Things are as they are."

"My mother must know. She will see the change in my feeling. And, Father, it has not changed. You say I deserve your sympathy. You are right that I do."

"Then let it all be known," said Hereward, throwing up his hands again. "Let them all start and stare and cast their stones. Let them do their part. It is what I am used to, what I have had. It is not what I have given, not what I will give. I will go on working and giving and suffering what I must. For I have suffered, Salomon. I am an unsatisfied man. I live with a want at my heart. You know now what that means."

"I am learning it, Father. And I have no wish to be revenged. You have done me no conscious wrong. But these secrets should not be. They lie beneath our life to escape and shatter it. They must be revealed and ended."

"Then end this one. Do as you will. Expose it in this house and the other. Let two families be shocked and saddened. It is your moment. They are all here. It is the usual treble gathering. Go and do your worst. Or your best, my boy. Go and do the only thing. We see it should be done."

"Not before Viola, Father. She must hear when she is alone. I will do it when I can."

"She is not with them," said Hereward, looking aside. "She is in my room. I was going to her there. She was to wait for me."

"Then I can go and do it now. It is the moment, as you say. You will break it to her yourself. In your room, where she is waiting for you. I said your path was clear."

Salomon almost ran from the room, paused on the threshold of the other, and stood with his hand raised.

"Hear me, all of you. I have a word to say. That is, there is a word to be said. You have heard others. This may or may not be the last. It is Viola who is involved this time. She should not have come amongst us. Do you guess what it is? Can you think what it might be? If so, I need not use the words."

"My son, what is it?" said Ada. "Surely there can be nothing more. Surely there has been enough."

"I think I can guess," said Alfred, coming forward. "This time I have felt I knew. At the early one I had no thought of it. Am I to say it, Ada? It is for you to judge."

"Say it, Father. Say anything that is true. Nothing is too much for me now. Too many things have been too much. It is silence that I cannot bear. It has covered too much. Let it not cover any more. It is the thing I cannot face."

"Then here is the truth. The last to come on us. This time I see it as the last. Viola is not the stranger we have thought. She is what she might naturally be. It is simply what might have been."

"I see, Father. You need not say it. We all know what it is. She is the child of Hereward and Emmeline, of my husband and my sister. We will say no more."

"My daughter, you have had much to face. But this is no new thing. Its place is in the past."

"My poor son!" said Ada, turning to Salomon. "This is not in the past for you. It is your trouble more than mine. For me the truth has been there, in a way a part of my life."

"Yes, it is so, Ada," said Emmeline. "There is nothing new. It is all so long ago. It has come to mean nothing. I felt it was best to hide the truth. Best for you and me and the child. I was going away, and it was easy to hide it. I thought I should never come back. And then it all seemed to be over, to be sunk in the past. And so it is. It is as you said. I did not think of this. How could anyone have thought of it?"

"There was a risk," said Alfred. "There is danger in hidden things. We see they have their life, that they do not die. There may be many of them. We do not know. We will not add to them. It is well that this has come to light. I have nothing to say of it. It is late to judge. It must join the knowledge behind our lives."

"Ada, I can go, if you wish," said Emmeline. "Tell me the truth. Do you want me to go or stay?"

"To stay. I need my sister. Nothing new has happened. No change has come. I simply have greater need. And Father wants his daughter—his grand-daughter—all that it is. I can accept it. If I had not learned to accept, I should be a person who could learn nothing."

"What a family we are!" said Reuben to his brothers. "I don't know whether to be proud or ashamed of belonging to it."

"I see no cause for pride," said Merton.

"I do," said Trissie, in a whisper. "They would make anyone proud. And I am almost their relation."

"I say nothing, Joanna," said Sir Michael. "Once more I wish you had not known. Once more I would have spared you."

"I say nothing too. I should like to say something in my own vein. Even at this moment I should like it. And I cannot think of anything. And I see I don't deserve to. Alfred was more fortunate. But then I daresay he did."

"Did you ever suspect this was the truth?"

"No, but I sometimes felt it ought to be. It fitted in like a book. And truth is stranger than fiction. So it ought to be as good."

"You all say that nothing has happened," said Zillah. "And you go on talking as if something had."

"You do not, Aunt Penelope," said Ada. "And I should like to have a word."

"Then you shall. I will say one. The word that had come into my mind. That I find you brave and kind and wise."

"Oh, Aunt Penelope, that is a help. It is just the word I need. It gives me strength to go on."

Sir Michael moved to Ada and put a hand on her shoulder. She started and broke into tears, and at that moment the door opened and Hereward stood with his eyes on her.

"So I have come at the peak of the occasion. I hoped it would be over. I thought I had given it time."

"It is over, Hereward," said Ada, raising her eyes. "And other things are over too. I shall say nothing. There is nothing for me to say."

"There is nothing for me either. The words would have no place. They are out of their time."

"Is this all it is to be?" said Joanna to her husband. "It somehow does not seem enough. I suppose I can't want it to be any more. It must be that human motives are mixed."

"So you have had a burden I did not know of, Hereward," said Ada. "As well as all those I know."

"My wife, it is a good word. It was a good thought. I do not meet so many. And there is a word I will say to you. And it has nothing to do with my daughter. I am glad you have given me my sons."

"So this has drawn Ada and Hereward together," said Joanna to Sir Michael. "It is always an unfortunate thing that does that. And it was unfortunate things that put them apart. I wonder if a fortunate thing could do anything. I have never heard of it."

"Joanna, I find it too much. Do not try to help me. Do not say we have another grandchild. I am degraded by these covert relationships. I am only sure of one thing. I wish my son had been different."

"In one way, Father," said Zillah. "Surely in no other. A man must be taken as a whole."

"Oh, this whole! It is a bale and a ban. Why must we take the whole of anything, when it is both good and bad? I can't help it, Joanna. I can only be myself."

"I don't want you to be anyone else. The standard is too uncertain. I must be able to respect my husband."

"I wish poor Ada could respect hers. I wish I could respect my son."

"I know you cannot, Father," said Hereward. "But you can take what I give. And I can respect you. Let that be the exchange between us. And this trouble is in the past."

"And when things are there, they do not count," said Joanna. " 'It is a long time ago' people say. So nothing is really wrong. It only has to wait long enough. It is a good thing this has done so."

"Mamma, you are what you are," said Ada. "I would not and could not say more."

"And I am what I am," said Sir Michael. "And I do not hear such words. But I can't help feeling there is right on my side."

"Of course there is," said Joanna. "There has to be right somewhere. Or there would not be such a thing. And there is not any anywhere else."

"Joanna, have we cared for Ada enough?" said Sir Michael, lowering his tone.

"We have not. She would never be cared for enough. Just as I am always cared for too much. Don't tell anyone I am proud of it."

"Well, you have never tried to achieve it."

"But I have. I have tried very hard. And I can feel I have my reward."

"Should we have a celebration to-night?" said Hereward, in an ironic tone. "There is nothing more to come to light. Is it an occasion to be observed?"

"Let us forget it and go on in our usual way," said Sir Michael, with something in his voice that did not exalt any other.

"Then we should send for Henry," said Salomon. "We have seen nothing of him since yesterday. That is not our usual way."

Henry appeared in response to the summons, and stood inside the room without evincing any sign of interest. Nurse had an air of uneasiness and remained at hand.

"He is not quite himself to-day, ma'am. He may be a little fractious. He had better not stay too long."

"Stay a long time," said Henry, in a tone that supported her misgiving.

"Come and talk to Father," said Hereward.

"No, not talk."

"Tell us what you have done to-day."

"No, not tell."

"Is it a secret?"

"No, not a secret. Secret is good."

"What has made you tired this evening?"

"Not tired. Not go upstairs. Not go to bed any more."

"But you would be tired then."

"Yes, he would, poor little boy," said Henry, wearily.

"Think of something you would like to do."

"Ring-a-ring-a-roses!" said Henry, a light breaking over his face.

The ensuing scene was a contrast to those that had preceded it. Galleon, alive to all of them, smiled to himself at the difference, while keeping in the background to avoid being involved.

"Well, I am the person to be tired," said Sir Michael, as he rose from the ground. "This is more for Henry's age than mine. I am three-quarters of a century too old for it."

"Grandpa very slow," said Henry looking at him.

"Yes, his bones are old and stiff. He can hear them creak."

Henry looked at him and broke into a wail.

"Poor Grandpa! His bones creak and he hear them. Hurt him very much."

"No, they are not hurting him now," said Nurse.

"Yes, he hear them. Henry hear them too. Oh, poor Grandpa!"

"No, you know you did not hear them."

"Not say he didn't hear," said Henry, angrily, as he was led from the room.

CHAPTER XIV

"Rosa, I am glad to be with you," said Hereward. "How long is it since we met?"

"I have lost count, as you have. Why are you with me now?"

"Does there have to be a reason?"

"No, but there is one. What has happened?"

"The one thing there was left to happen. My last secret has escaped. I must talk of it to someone. There has to be silence at home."

"You are fortunate. There might be something else. Does Salomon want to marry Viola?"

"Rosa, you think of it at once. How did you guess?"

"Well, he is the one who is free. And she is what we know. It seems a situation for your family."

"I should not have kept the secret. I am learning the value of truth."

"It might not have seemed to have so much value at the time."

"If I had married you, Rosa, these things would not have happened."

"Other things would. They did happen. Our relation was one of them."

"My poor boy! My selfless, dependable son! The girl is less on my mind. I almost feel I came first with her."

"Hereward, how far did you go?"

"As far as I should, and no further. Who should have a greater care for her? And I can guard against women's feelings for me."

"You might have put the power to better use. But you have used other powers, Hereward. You have served many."

"My heart goes out in sympathy and pity," said Hereward, moving about the room. "My strongest instinct is to ease the human way. I see it as a long, hard journey. I take no credit for it. It is my way of fulfilling myself. I ask no gratitude. And perhaps I hardly have it. It is felt it means no sacrifice. And it has meant none. I am not made up of failings. And those I have, come from my strength."

"What a satisfactory reason for them! Mine come from something else."

"You could have held me, Rosa. Something in you would have done it, something in yourself."

"It would have worn thin. You would have come to the end of it."

"But I have not done so. It is always there for me."

"It is there when you are with me. That is not always. It is very seldom."

"From the first I saw the whole of my wife. I do not mean there is little to see. She is larger-hearted than many. And there is other largeness in her. But she is herself and nothing more."

"You say you saw the whole of her. How much did you see? How much did she see of you? She may have realised her largeness of heart and felt you would both need it. And it seems you have done so."

"It is true. But her life has been a full one. And I feel she knows it."

"I have no doubt of it. It could hardly have escaped her."

"You and she might have had a friendship, if you had come together. But it seemed it should not be."

"It did. You could hardly betray yourself before your marriage."

"Would you have liked to have sons?"

"I suppose I should. I see people do like it."

"You would not like the position of my wife?"

"The words can have two meanings. On the whole I should not."

"On the whole Ada does."

"Well, she is large-hearted. I think my heart must be only of average size."

"You can't think that average is the word for you."

"Not on the whole. No one thinks that of himself. If anyone did, we should sometimes meet it."

"I believe we meet it in Ada. She does not see herself as above the average."

"But she knows how rare that is. It is a way of feeling she is above it."

"I am grateful to her, Rosa. Do not think I am not. But I might have been grateful to you."

"I don't want gratitude. It is earned too hardly. And people do not give enough."

"Perhaps not. But I have tried to give it. I believe my wife has found it all worth while."

"Some of it has been so. She has taken the rough with the smooth. I should have been inclined to reject the rough. I don't know why it always has to be included."

"Well, I have a good wife, Rosa, dear sons, grand-children coming. But I hoped to have them through you. And to-day I feel I must imagine it. It is not often in my thought."

"It hardly ever is. So do not put it into mine. I have no place for it."

"So you really never feel regret?"

"You think I should imagine what might have been? We found I had not a large heart. Now you must find I have not much imagination."

"In me it is the force of my life. And to-day it is working on you."

"What do you mean? You don't want to use me in a book?"

"You would not recognise yourself. Would you not be glad to be of help to me?"

"I am seldom glad to be of help. The gladness would not be on my side. And we are supposed not to write about a person until the deep feeling is past. So that is what it is."

"Rosa, I gave you a book before I was married. With a farewell poem on the flyleaf. If you have it, will you lend it to me? It would be of help."

"I will give it to you. It is yours. It holds something for you and nothing for me. You can put it to your own use."

Hereward accepted the book, and soon afterwards took his leave. He seemed ready to be gone, as if his thought was pressing forward. His companion let him go and did not look after him.

When he reached his house, he left the book in the hall while he changed his clothes. Ada and Salomon entered from outside, and Ada took up the book and glanced at it.

"What is this? The poem that is written here? What does it mean?"

"Yes, I see it, Mother. It means or has meant what it says. It may mean nothing now. The years have passed."

"Your poor father! I have wondered what he did before we were married. It seems there must have been something."

"Considering what he did afterwards? Yes, there must have been. I have wondered too. Well, it seems it was no bad thing."

"My poor Hereward! I was not the woman for him. So I was not even then."

"Mother, was he the man for you? Is that someone you have not known? Perhaps that was equal between you. And you have come to a fair end."

"Other things have not been equal. And there have been things before the end. I do not forget them. I never shall. And there are others who will not forget. But we will not speak of the poem to your father. It was not written for our eyes."

"Or it would not have told us so much. And it tells us something more. The woman it was written for has parted with it. And to the man who wrote it and gave it. Perhaps we are told enough."

As they entered the library, Hereward followed with Henry in his arms, having met him as he came from the garden. The latter carried the book, and seemed content with his possession of it.

"Read," he said as his father sat down.

"No, you read to us," said Hereward.

Henry leant towards the book and appeared held by its words.

> " 'Ride a cock horse
> To Banbury Cross,' "

he said, as if struck by them.

"Well, go on, or do you forget?"

"Not forget. Book not tell any more."

"No, say what is true," said Nurse. "You often forget just there! 'And see a fine lady—' "

" 'Get on a white horse'," said Henry, in a painstaking tone, his eyes close to the page.

"There is something written on the blank leaf," said Sir Michael. "It looks like a poem."

"That is what it is," said Hereward. "An effort of my youth. Not to be regarded or revealed."

"I did not know you wrote poetry."

"I don't. And I have realised it. I found it was not what I wrote."

Sir Michael made a movement to take the book, but Henry forestalled him.

"No, not Grandpa's. Take it upstairs. Henry's own book."

"Well, perhaps you can have it," said Nurse, with a glance at Hereward. "But you would like to hear a story first."

"Once upon a time," said Henry, urgently, turning to his father.

Hereward rose to the effort, and as Henry became absorbed, received the book from Nurse and put it in his pocket.

CHAPTER XV

"Good-morning, Sir Hereward," said Galleon.

"Oh, good-morning. So that is what you call me now. I had forgotten about it."

"It will have to be remembered, Sir Hereward. The change has taken place."

"It is only a nominal change. It will not affect myself."

"Well, that is as you feel, Sir Hereward."

"My life and my work will go on. The difference will only be in name."

"Names are an indication, Sir Hereward. And this is something further."

"You feel that work and a title do not go together?"

"Well, there tends to be a gulf, Sir Hereward."

"This is a very small title."

"As old as the Tudors, Sir Hereward, I am told."

"And a writer may be a man without a background?"

"Well, it is as you say, Sir Hereward."

"I meant it was as you would say."

"There was no need for me to take it upon myself, Sir Hereward."

"You would respect me more, if I did nothing?"

"On the contrary, Sir Hereward. There are duties in every sphere."

"My eldest son represents me. He is my deputy."

"Yes, Sir Hereward. It can only be the word."

"We need the money that I earn."

Galleon paused and then just inclined his head.

"You think that is not a subject for words?"

"It is not always seen as one, Sir Hereward."

"You feel the fact is a thing to be ashamed of?"

"It is a chance circumstance, Sir Hereward."

"We could hardly have kept things up, if I had done nothing."

"These places have their life, Sir Hereward. It involves the power of holding to it."

"They can lose their life. In a measure they depend on money!"

"You are not of a stock that looks to it, Sir Hereward. There are other standards."

"But everything has to be paid for."

"It is true that the world is run on that basis, Sir Hereward."

"And does our corner not belong to it?"

"It is perhaps apart in more than one sense, Sir Hereward."

"You feel that I fail it in some way?"

"Well, perhaps that you withdraw from it, Sir Hereward."

"Won't you get tired of using my name?"

"No, Sir Hereward. The question would not arise."

"I shall get rather tired of hearing it."

"It will cease to strike your ear, Sir Hereward. Good-morning, my lady."

Joanna entered the room by herself, a reminder of how seldom she had done so. She was dressed as usual, but her look was unfamiliar. Her son went to meet her and take her to a seat.

"Mamma, this is brave and wise. The first steps have to be taken. It is like you to know it."

"It would be like most of us. How can we help knowing?"

"At the moment you wish you had no more to take."

"No, I wish both your father and I had more."

"I know what it is to you to be here without him."

"Well, it is the alternative to being nowhere."

"You are feeling he is the more fortunate?"

"No, I suppose I am. But it is not the word."

"We all have to die in our time. There is no escape."

"When we have had to be alive. And when the two things are so different. We ought not to have to do both."

"It is true, my lady, if I may interpose," said Galleon. "The one does not help with the other. It seems to render it unnatural."

"And in spite of that it leads to it. The position is unreasonable."

Ada came into the room, and at once turned her eyes on her mother-in-law.

"Mamma, it is what I expected. I meet what I knew I should. May I do as well, when my times comes."

"Perhaps you may escape it," said Hereward. "A man may outlive his wife. It is a thing that happens."

"Not as often as the other thing. It is the woman who is left. Women marry younger, and on the whole have longer lives. It is no advantage to them."

"I think it is," said Joanna. "And I am one of them."

"In a sense you hardly are. You are so much one by yourself. And your courage does not deceive us. We know what is in your mind. That you have come to the end. But you are too brave to allow yourself to betray it."

"People are always brave in trouble. How can they be anything else? It is brave of them to suffer it."

"Dear Mamma! You are feeling there is nothing left for you."

"I do feel there is only a little left."

"You will live in the past. That will always be your own."

"I have lived in it. But then it was the present. And that was much better."

"There is the future," said Ada, raising her hands, "the great, unforeseeable future. With its hopes and fears, its demands and its duties. You are to have a share of it."

"It does not sound so very good. But I daresay it would not. This was once the future."

"Well, we are now in the present," said Hereward.

"And we all have our duty to that. I must go and attend to mine."

"No, you must not, Hereward," said Ada. "You must remain with your mother. No duty is as pressing as that to-day. An exception can sometimes be made. And Galleon is here with the breakfast. Are we to live on air?"

"You may have feared it, my lady. I have had to assert myself. Trouble is taken to mean that life has not to go on."

"Well, it ought to mean it," said Joanna. "It should be allowed to prevent it."

"Oh, that is what I am called now!" said Ada, as if taken aback. "I am not sure that I like it. No, I find I do not. It is someone else's appellation, not mine. I had forgotten, and I shall continue to forget."

"Other people will remember, my lady. The change cannot be denied."

"But then there will be two of us. How is that to be arranged? If the title is mine, and I suppose it is, what of the accepted bearer of it?"

"Joanna, Lady Egerton, my lady," said Galleon, evenly.

"I am too old to have a Christian name," said Joanna.

"Then you shall not have one," said Ada. "You shall be what you have always been. And I know the thought in your mind. The name was for Papa's lips and for his alone. And so it shall be to the end. It does not matter what I am. I will be anything that comes about. I have no claim, or anyhow I make none."

"There is no choice, my lady. And the name is not used in speech."

"Oh, how we are all under orders! We in the land of the free! Well, we must submit, I suppose. If the change must come, it must."

"We have made enough of it," said Hereward. "It is no such great one."

"It is a mark of the change in our lives. And that is a great one. It will be a shock to Merton. I have sent the message."

"He and his wife are in the hall," said Hereward, who now spoke of Hetty in this way.

"Ah, he would come to his mother. My son, I had to send a sad word. Yes, go first to your grandmother. She is the claimant to-day. All our thought centres round her. We take a secondary place."

"Now this is a relief!" said Merton. "I looked to be without grandparents. Things are only half as bad as I expected. I did not know that could happen. I feel it is too much."

"And so it is. She comes out high. You must see that her grandsons are worthy of her.—Father, I knew you would be here. Aunt Penelope, I looked for this. It is what we can do for each other. To be ourselves as far as we can."

"I suppose I am being myself," said Reuben. "But I half-felt we ought to be different."

"So did I," said Salomon. "I felt my ordinary self was not enough."

"Hereward may not quite come up to himself," went on Ada. "You may find him a thought aloof and silent. I think we must look for it to-day. His mind is on the past."

"Mine is being held to the present," said Merton.

"Well, I will take my cue," said Hereward. "My wife will fulfil a double part."

"Well, it is what my hand findeth to do. So I do it with my might. These are difficult moments at the best. And a general silence would not serve. I don't know why we feel a sort of uneasiness and guilt, when we have lost someone near to us. But so it is. There is no eluding it."

"I know why," said Salomon. "We are uneasy at the proof that we can die, and guilty because we have not died, when someone else has. It seems ungenerous of us."

"Well, we must just get through the time as best we can."

"And that is as we see," said Merton.

"And it might be worse," said Salomon. "If it were left to us, it would be. What are we doing?"

"Nothing. And it is not worse."

"I think it is," said Reuben. "I am feeling ashamed of it."

"Father, step into the breach," said Ada. "Someone must second my efforts. My powers are giving out. They are not unlimited."

"Do not give a sigh of relief," said Reuben to Merton. "We should have to hear it."

"I have lost an old and dear friend," said Alfred. "Your husband has lost his father. And his mother has the greatest loss. What else is there to be said?"

"Nothing, Father. But it is a help to hear you say it. It becomes simple and natural, coming from your lips. It seems to lose its mystery and threat. And his mother is true to herself. I cannot tell you to what height she has risen. It leaves us impressed and silent."

"Don't say it has not done the last," said Reuben. "Again we should have to hear."

"And now, Aunt Penelope, something from you. We are not to be without it."

"I will say it to the one with the greatest loss," said Penelope, moving to Joanna.

"Ah, right again. Your instinct never fails. You cannot do better than follow it."

"We know no one wants us, Ada," said Emmeline. "But we felt we wanted everyone. So we have come with nothing to say and no help to give."

"But with a touch of the old charm," said Ada, caressing her cheek. "I don't mean it is not often there. But it must become intermittent, with the other echoes of youth. We are grateful for any return of it. We are having all we can."

"I am not," said Hereward to Viola. "Where is the chance for us to have anything? Our relationship is seen as a reason for keeping us apart. It is an unusual view of it."

"It is the relationship that is seen as unusual. But in the end it will be accepted. We will go slowly and not expect too much. And gradually expect more and more."

"And in the end expect the whole," said Hereward, in a distinct tone, glancing about him. "I will have what is mine."

"People feel it strange that life goes on, when someone has died," said Zillah. "But does it go on? There seems to be little sign of it."

"You notice the pause more than I do," said Salomon. "So much of my life is pause."

"Now are we accepting the pause too much?" said Ada. "Is there an element of self-indulgence in it? We must be on our guard against the temptations of grief. They exist in that state as in any other."

"I wish I knew what they were," said Joanna. "So that I could yield to them."

"Mamma, through everything you remain your original and immutable self. You are a beacon in the darkness, something to point our way. You remind me of a lighthouse, solitary itself, but sending forth light. Now do you not all agree with me? Is there a dissentient voice?"

"It would be a bold one," said Merton.

"And a wicked one," said Reuben.

"It would be both," said Salomon. "Of course it is noble to endure grief. Not being able to help it makes it nobler. It would be different if we chose it."

"Zillah, you did not mind my taking the office of eulogist upon myself? It might be held to be the part of the daughter. But feeling took hold of me, and I was carried away. And I know I have your support."

"You have. And I am going to ask for yours. I am about to adopt the character myself. Not on behalf of my mother. That has been done. On that of my brother and your husband. Is there not a beacon there, a light to point our way? Something solitary itself, sending forth light? If his failings are on the scale of himself, on what other scale should they be? Has not the time come to know him, to see him as he is? To see ourselves as we are, and in our dealings with him. I will not ask for an answer. There is none, as there is only one. I will say your own words to you. I have taken the office of eulogist upon myself. It might be held to be the part of the wife. But feeling took hold of me, and I was carried away. And I can echo you again. Is there a dissentient voice?"

"There should not be one at all," murmured Reuben. "Suppose it was dissentient?"

"How father's failings add to him!" said Merton. "I join in the respectful admission of their scale. I am ashamed of my own petty faults."

"I don't think I have any," said Reuben. "Or I can't think of them. They must be on a scale too mean to gain my attention."

"I can only think I am perfect," said Salomon. "People say how trying a perfect person would be. And we see they are right."

"Well, I have my part to play," said Hereward. "We are grateful for tribute, and our gratitude is sincere. But I have had to thank my sister for too much, to thank her further now. It is not for me to agree with her, or to presume to disagree. I will say I have done my best. And my worst, if it must be said. I can hardly wish I had done more. I wish some things were undone. But they have brought their good."

"Father, is your silence to persist?" said Ada. "It may seem to you natural, even fitting to-day. But your voice is always welcome."

"You hardly encourage me to use it."

"Now you know what I mean. I do not think feelings should be hidden. I have never subscribed to that school of thought. Anything that is there must give its signs. Anything does, as far as I have seen. But we will accept your silence as a sign, if that is what it is. Aunt Penelope will represent you."

"I will ask for silence to serve me in the same way."

"I am nervous," said Reuben. "Lest I should be giving signs."

"I am nervous lest I should not be giving them," said Solomon. "I can only half-hope I am."

"I am nervous lest everyone should begin to give them," said Merton. "I hardly dare to see and hear."

"And now, Hereward?" said Ada. "You can't have nothing more to say."

"There is nothing more to be said. The part of an echo is not mine."

"Hereward, that is unworthy of you. You know what you would make of all this, if you were conceiving a book. You are an adept at letting things grow under your hand and become larger than life. It is held to be your strong point."

"Life is enough in itself to-day. It does not need my service."

"Oh, there it is again! My words are misinterpreted, and my thought with them, I had better be silent."

"A safe choice," murmured Merton.

"Now why?" said his mother, turning to him. "Would it do for everyone to be mum and mute, and self-indulgent in the way that goes with grief? Ah, every state has its snares, and we should remember them. And saying nothing may mean that people have nothing to say."

"Then it is hard to see how they can see it."

"Well, they don't, my dear, as we can see. But the excuse does not apply to your father. Even this argument could be material for him."

"You said I was expert at making things larger than life," said Hereward. "I should have to depend on the gift."

"You might make it smaller than life," said Merton. "So that it could reach vanishing point."

"Now I knew you could talk, if you liked. Not that your speeches had so much to recommend them. Mamma, you have not made one."

"No, and she will not," said Hereward.

"Of course she will not, if she does not wish to. What a tone to take over something that goes without saying! Do you suppose that pressure would be brought to bear on her? Salomon, say a word to your father to bring him to a state of reason."

"Here is one that is workaday enough. I am doing the accounts, and some of the rents have not come in. Two of the farmers', and one other. They are a good deal behind with them."

"I know the men you mean," said Hereward. "I have waived the rent of one, and given the other more time. These are not easy days for them. Rosa Lindsay's rent comes through me. I must give it to you."

"Rosa!" said Ada. "Oh, yes, the name! Yes, of course. Rosa Lindsay. Is she not an old tenant?"

"Yes, and an old friend. I sometimes see her."

"Why does she send the rent through you? She must know that Salomon does the accounts."

"Must she? I don't know how or why. I have not told her."

"You must talk about something when you are with her."

"That is true. But there are other topics. We should not be at a loss for them."

"No. There would be many. You must both remember the past."

"What do you mean? Oh, the book that was in the hall! You saw it and read the poem? Well, it did me no discredit. Or none on moral grounds."

"I suppose the relation is now a formal one?"

"No, its roots are too deep. It dates from before my marriage."

"I wonder it did not end in it."

"Some people thought it would. For a time I was one of them."

"Why did you not propose to her? You had the matter in your hands."

"I took it into them. But it was also in hers."

There was a pause.

"I suppose I should be grateful to her. So she determined the course of my life."

"There is no need. She had no thought of it."

"And you turned to the second best. I wonder if I have realised it. I think in a way I have."

"Ada, I have not regretted it. I hope on the whole you have not."

"I wonder you charge her any rent, when there is that between you. Oh, I daresay you don't. Do you provide it yourself?"

"You seem to have your thoughts on the matter. You can decide."

"Is the rent paid by cheque, Salomon?"

"No, I think it comes in money."

"Then your father does provide it. Only cottagers pay in coin. Does it always come in that way?"

"You are talking to my father, Mother. I hardly remember how everything comes."

"You remember how this does. Well, there is no reason why he should not help someone who needs it."

"None," said her husband. "I have never seen any. If I had, my life would have been different. And not only mine. I am as I am. That is why you and your sons are as you are. I need not say it again. You know the truth."

"Oh, I do, Hereward. You have not hidden it. It is not the kind of thing you hide."

"No, do not say it again," said Alfred. "You are as you are, and it is why my daughter and her sons are as they are. Yes, we know the truth. I need not say it again either. I shall never say it again. I will say nothing more to-day. We will have a word with your mother and take our leave."

Hereward gave no sign and accompanied them to the hall. And at first his family were silent.

"It is not strange that Father admires himself through everything," said Merton. "It is what most of us do. It is strange that he does it openly. Most of us would not dare."

"It shows we don't really admire ourselves," said Salomon. "He has the courage of conviction."

"I don't think I admire myself at all," said Ada. "Perhaps not even as much as I might."

"I don't think I even might," said Trissie, who had been silent.

"I daresay there is not much to admire. But I doubt if most people have much more."

"I think they have less," said Trissie.

"So do I," said the three brothers.

"Oh, how worth while you make it seem! How worth while you make it in itself! I would not go back and unlive it. The good has outweighed the bad."

"I felt it would," said Hereward, in a quiet tone, as he returned. "I meant it should. I look back without regret. I do not see myself as a god."

"Then how does he see himself?" murmured Salomon. "None but a god could be as he is, and remain exalted in all our eyes. Literature and legend prove it. And feeling for children is known to go with divine powers. Here is someone who illustrates it."

"Raining," said Henry, in an incidental tone, as he entered the room.

"We had only gone a few steps when it began," said Nurse.

"Not a few," said Henry, looking down at his feet, as if in concern for them.

"Anyhow you did not get wet."

"He did," said Henry, passing his hands down his coat.

"Only a few drops," said Nurse.

"No, not a few."

"So you don't like the rain," said Ada.

"Yes, he does. Very nice rain. Henry heard it."

"But you did not have your walk."

"No, it rained," said Henry, contentedly.

"Come and tell Father about it," said Hereward.

Henry went towards him, glanced at Joanna as he passed, and came to a pause.

"Poor Grandma very tired this morning."

"Yes, she is. You must not trouble her."

"Play game," said Henry, observing the size of the gathering, and suggesting a beneficial course.

"No, we want to be quiet to-day."

"Grandpa play," said Henry, looking round the room.

"No, Grandpa is not here this morning."

"Grandma want him," said Henry, in a tone of remonstrance.

"Yes, she does. But he cannot come to her. He has been too ill."

"Henry read to him. Then quite well again," said Henry, ending on a rising note.

"Yes, he liked you to read," said Hereward. "You will always be able to remember it."

"Yes, Father play," said Henry, finding the attitude amenable.

"No, we are not thinking of games to-day."

"Not a nice day?" suggested Henry, seeking a reason for the blankness.

"Come and let us tell you about Maud," said Merton.

"Very good girl. Not stamp and cry. Not at all spoilt," said Henry, openly forestalling information.

"What shall we tell her about you?" said Hetty.

"Send her his love," said Henry, in a tone of ending the matter.

"A letter, my lady," said Galleon, offering a salver to Ada.

"Grandma my lady," said Henry looking at them.

"And one for you, Sir Hereward."

"One for you, *sir*," corrected Henry.

"He does not miss much," said Galleon.

"Oh, yes, he knows everything," said Henry.

"I think they have had enough of you," said Nurse.

Henry turned to Hereward and climbed on his knee.

"Whom do you love?" said Hereward.

"Galleon," said Henry, with feeling. "And dear Grandpa best."

"You will not see Grandpa again," said Hereward, in a quiet tone.

"Oh, no," said Henry, easily.

"You will not forget him, will you?"

"See him tomorrow. Not forget."

"It is no good, Sir Hereward," said Nurse. "He is too young to understand."

"Only say *sir*," said Henry, with some impatience.

"He likes the old order," said Hereward.

"He is wise," said Salomon. "There seems little to be said for the end of it."

"Ah, my dear father! We saw things and thought of them differently. But at heart we were at one. A part of myself and my life is torn away."

"Poor Father!" said Henry, looking up at him.

"Yes, poor Father! But it is poor Grandma most of all."

Henry got down and went to Joanna, patted her knee and looked up into her face, doing what he could to compensate her.

"Grandma better now?" he suggested, hardly confident of his success.

"Yes, you have made me feel better."

"But not well; no. Henry tell her something."

"What have you to tell me?"

"Once upon a time there was a little boy," said Henry, after a pause.

"And is that the whole of the story?"

"Yes. Not any more."

"Well, now we can go upstairs," said Nurse.

"No. Show her the picture. Quite safe in your bag. Draw it himself."

"Oh, yes, in my reticule," said Nurse, accustomed to interpreting primitive speech. "Yes, I will leave you to show it to your grandmamma."

Henry took the sheet of paper in both his hands, looked at it for a long moment, and displayed it.

"So you have made a picture," said Joanna. "What is it meant to be?"

"It is still raining, my lady. It is meant to be a horse. I hardly think it will stop to-day," said Nurse, in an even, incidental tone, without turning her head.

"Why, it is a horse!" said Hereward. "Why, so it is."

"Yes," said Henry, smiling. "It has legs."

"And is that the tail?"

"No tail," said Henry, who had not thought to put one.

"Well, we will give him one. There it is."

"Yes," said Henry, smiling again. "Henry did it."

"Oh, what would Nurse say? You know it was Father."

Henry turned and showed the picture to Joanna.

"Horse and tail," he said, choosing words that did not commit him.

"Oh, how clever you are!"

"Yes," said her grandson.

"And where is the horse's mane?"

Henry attempted to depict it, regarded the result, and suddenly tore the paper across.

"The despair of the creator!" said Merton.

"A feeling known to Merton," said Reuben.

"It is," said his brother. "It will never be known to you. And it can be beyond us."

"Oh, what a waste of your work!" said Hereward to Henry.

"The feeling is not known to Father," said Salomon.

"No, it is not," said Merton, and was silent.

"Would you like to be destroyed?" said Zillah to Henry. "Perhaps the horse did not like it."

"He did," said Henry, looking away. "And Henry made him."

"The god-like spirit," said Salomon. "He creates life and destroys it. His father's son."

"Draw again," said Henry to Joanna, and receiving another piece of paper, began to do so.

"You will learn to draw when you are older," said Hereward.

"Yes, to-morrow," said Henry, not looking up.

"He will have to learn other things," said Merton to his brothers. "Things of another kind. Who he is, who we all are, and what some of us might be. There may be breakers ahead."

"That is enough," said Salomon. "What a thing to talk about to-day! Father is looking at you."

"And hearing him," said Hereward, quietly. "And it is true that the time is ill-chosen."

"The truth is in our minds," said Merton. "It is one that should never leave them. It may bear on coming lives."

"Not to their harm, if we have a care."

"Some things are out of our hands."

"This one will be in mine."

"It is time for us to go," said Hetty, who, as always, had been watching Henry. "Maud and her nurse are calling for us. I hear them in the hall."

"They can come in for a moment," said Hereward. "And we can see if there are signs of danger."

Merton's daughter entered, glanced at Henry and stood in silence. Henry returned the glance and looked away.

"Say good-morning to Great-Grandma," said Merton. Maud remained silent.

"Come, surely you can say a word."

"Pencil," said Maud, looking at Henry's occupation.

The latter did not raise his eyes, and Maud's also maintained their direction.

"Let her have the pencil, Henry," said Ada. "She is younger than you, and she is your guest."

Henry put it smoothly behind his back.

"Come, the house must be full of pencils," said Hereward, glancing at his son.

Maud looked round for signs of this, and seeing none, made an advance on the pencil and acquired it.

Her host broke down.

"Come, what a way to behave!" said Ada.

"Paper," said Maud.

Zillah produced a sheet and another pencil; the nurses assigned them to their charges; and the latter turned their backs on each other and gave themselves to their art.

"Well, there seems no need for anxiety," said Hereward.

"None at this moment," said Merton. "It is one that has no meaning."

"It bears on others. I shall watch them as they come."

"Don't you want to see Henry's picture?" said Hetty to Maud, feeling that egotism should have its limits.

"No, see Maud's," said the latter, in whom it had none.

"Look at Maud's picture, Henry," said Ada.

Henry gave a glance in its direction and returned to his own.

"We should be going, ma'am," said Maud's nurse. "Maud come home to her pretty toys."

Maud pursued what she felt to be her calling.

"We must take your picture home or Henry will want it," said the nurse, putting the virtue of necessity before any other.

Maud accepted this likelihood, gathered up her acquisitions and was borne away.

"We don't make enough of Maud," said Ada.

"You don't make anything of her," said Merton. "Henry fills your eyes."

"Not mine. Maud is my own grandchild. It has been an effort to make no difference."

"You have failed in a sense you do not mean."

"Well, Henry is in the house," said Hereward.

"He is, at all times and in all parts of it."

"Merton, you are a father yourself."

"I am, and I am reminding you of it."

"Would you like to have Maud to tea?" said Ada, bending to Henry.

"No," said the latter, keeping his eyes on his work.

"But you always like to see her."

"Take Henry's pencil," said Henry, after a pause.

"But you were glad for her to have it."

"No," said Henry, looking up.

"Henry has a future," said Merton. "Do you ever give a thought to it?"

"Oh, surely the time is not yet," said Hereward.

"The early steps lead to others. They would be better on the right path. He will have to grow up and marry like everyone else."

"Marry," murmured Henry to himself.

"Have a wife to live with you," said Hereward. "Whom would you like to have?"

"Dear little Maud," said Henry, in a tone of ending the matter to everyone's content.